Learn Mobile Game Development in One Day Using Gamesalad

Create Games for iOS, Android, and Windows Phones and Tablets

Jamie Cross

Learn Mobile Game Development in One Day Using Gamesalad

ISBN-13: 978-1511914208
ISBN-10: 1511914203

Trademarks

Trademarked names, logos, and images may appear in this book. Rather than use a trademark symbol with every occupance of a trademarked name, logo, or image the author used the names, logos, and images only in a editorial fashion and to the benefit of the trademark owner, with no intention of infringement of the trademark.

The use in this book of trade name, trademarks, service marks, and similar terms, even if they are not identified as such, is not to be taken as an expression of opinion as to whether or not they are subject to proprietary rights.

Gamesalad is a trademark of Gamesalad Inc.
Macintosh is a trademark of Apple, Inc.
Windows is a trademark of Microsoft Corp.
All other trademarks are the property of their respective owners.

Credits

Some assets used in the creation of some of the games within this book are used under creative commons license or have been placed in the public domain.

» Artwork by MillionthVector (millionthvector.blogspot.com) is licensed under a Creative Commons Attribution 4.0 International License.
» Artwork by Kenney (Kenney.nl) is placed in the public domain.
» Artwork from Glitch (glitchthegame.com) is placed in the public domain.

Table of Contents

Preface

Preface

This book has been written so readers will get up to speed and quickly learn how to work with Gamesalad to quickly and easily develop 2D mobile video games. Readers will not only learn how to create four specific game types, but will learn about game development in general. In addition to creating four different games, while working through the exercises in this book, readers will not only learn how to use Gamesalad, but will be taught why things work the way they do. When you have finished reading this book, you will have a solid understanding of game development using Gamesalad and have four mobile-ready games to publish.

Who Should Read This Book

This book is for anyone who wants to learn how to create their own video games for desktop and mobile devices using Gamesalad. While this is an introductory book that assumes you have no previous game development experience, you'll find that once you have completed all of the chapters and exercises, you'll be able to create your own amazing video games from scratch.

Overview of Chapters

This book is written in a series of 24 chapters representing the 24 hours in one day. Each chapter should take approximately an hour to complete.

» **Chapter 1:** Introduction to Game Development with Gamesalad—This chapter will introduce you to game development and show you how to download and install Gamesalad.

» **Chapter 2:** The Scenes Tab and The Stage—In this chapter, you will learn about the stage and how to add scenes to a game.

» **Chapter 3:** Game Objects and Gamesalad's Coordinate System—This chapter will teach you about Gamesalad's coordinate system and introduce you to actors, one of the main components of Gamesalad.

» **Chapter 4:** Actors and Their Attributes—You will learn more details about actors and how to create, set up, and use them in a game.

» **Chapter 5:** Game 1—Pachinko/Plinko—It's time for your first game. In this chapter, you'll use what you've learned to create one of the most popular games in the world!

» **Chapter 6:** Attributes—In this chapter, you'll be introduced to attributes, Gamesalad's way of dealing with variables. You'll not only learn how to use Gamesalad's built-in attributes, but learn how to create and manipulate your own custom attributes.

» **Chapter 7:** Graphics and Artwork—This chapter will teach you all about creating graphics for use in Gamesalad. You'll learn what file types to use, how to create your art at the correct size, and how to create a transparent background for sprites.

» **Chapter 8:** Behaviors Part 1–In chapter 8, you'll be introduced to behaviors, Gamesalad's drag and drop coding language. You'll learn the basics of using behaviors and see just how easy it is to create your own custom games.

» **Chapter 9:** Behaviors Part 2–This chapter continues the discussion about behaviors by focusing on some of the "special" behaviors Gamesalad offers.

» **Chapter 10:** Player Input–You'll learn several ways to accept input from the player in chapter 10, from creating keyboard controls to accepting touch input on mobile devices.

» **Chapter 11:** Game 2—Space Shooter–For the second game, you'll create a classic 80's style arcade game, pitting the player against an endless onslaught of alien space fighters.

» **Chapter 12:** Audio–In chapter 12, you will learn how to add and use music and sound effects in your Gamesalad projects.

» **Chapter 13:** The Expression Editor–This chapter will teach you the "ins and outs" of the expression editor, Gamesalad's tool for adding formulas to games. You'll learn how to manipulate both mathematic and text formulas using the expression editor.

» **Chapter 14:** Collisions and Physics–In this chapter, you'll learn how to create collision shapes and how to manipulate the physics settings of each actor so you can create complex actor interactions.

» **Chapter 15:** Camera Control and Graphical User Interfaces–Chapter 15 will show you how to control the game's camera, the player's window to your game world, and how to create and set up common graphical user interface (GUI) elements.

» **Chapter 16:** Game 3—Box Breaker–Time for game 3! In this game, you'll use all of the knowledge you have gathered to create a physics-based puzzle game.

» **Chapter 17:** Animation and Particles–In chapter 17, you'll learn how to animate, in Gamesalad, using frame-based cells and built-in behaviors. You'll also examine how to create spectacular particle effects using the particles behavior.

» **Chapter 18:** Tables–This chapter will teach you all about tables, Gamesalad's way of collecting and organizing large amounts of information. You will learn how to create tables, edit them, and recall their data for use by actors.

» **Chapter 19:** Game Polish–This chapter teaches the importance of polishing and play testing your games. It also examines the role a consistent game style plays in development.

» **Chapter 20:** Game 4—Geometry Runner–For your fourth and final game, you'll create a pulse pounding, non-stop endless runner style game.

» **Chapter 21:** Mobile Development–Chapter 21 will show you how to configure your development environment for mobile games. You'll learn how to play test on mobile devices and learn more details about how to create interactions with mobile games.

» **Chapter 22:** Publishing–In this chapter, you will learn how to use Gamesalad's publishing portal to publish games for desktop computers, mobile devices, and even as browser-based HTML 5 games.

» **Chapter 23:** Improving The Games–This chapter will show you how to make some improvements to the four games you have created throughout the book and prepare them for mobile distribution.

» **Chapter 24:** Review and Resources–In this chapter, you will review everything you have learned while reading this book and look at some additional resources you can use to continue with Gamesalad and game development.

Gamesalad Creator Version and Platform

This book was written using the Macintosh version of Gamesalad Creator version number 0.12.10. Gamesalad Creator is available for both the Macintosh and Windows platforms and while the interface on each platform is somewhat different, they both share the same capabilities and benefits. The screen shots used throughout this book have been taken from the Macintosh version, so the individual screens will look different if you are a Windows user. However, all of the game development concepts remain the same and the same games can be created and played on either platform.

Free vs. Paid Gamesalad Creator

Gamesalad offers two "versions" of Creator: a free (Basic) version and a paid (Pro) version. To get the most out of this book, you don't need anything more than the free Basic version of Gamesalad. The free version contains everything you will need to complete this book and even make your own commercial-quality games for distribution on the Apple iOS App Store. If you are curious about the specific differences between the Basic and Pro versions of Gamesalad, there are full details on the two licenses at the Gamesalad website (http://gamesalad.com/creator/pro#pricing).

About the Author

Jamie Cross, a graphic designer that has been working in the field for nearly 25 years, is currently a partner at Clay Communications, a graphic design studio located near Pittsburgh, PA.

In addition to graphic design, Jamie has been involved in computer programming, of one kind or another, since the age of 16 when he got his first Commodore 64 computer. At that time, he programmed in BASIC. He now has experience in several languages including Java, HTML, JavaScript, and Lua; however, the bulk of his game development is done using Gamesalad Creator.

Jamie has published several games to the Apple App Store. He teaches game development online, has written articles about game development for the tuts+ network of websites, and runs his own website and YouTube channel with lots of information about Gamesalad Creator and game development in general.

Conventions

Throughout this book you will find a number of text styles that distinguish between different kinds of information. Here is an example and an explanation of their meaning.

Important words or concepts will be highlighted with a capital letter when I am specifically instructing you to interact with that item on screen, like this: "navigate to the Scene Tab".

When you are being instructed to perform a specific action it will be highlighted in bold text, like this: "Add a Timer Behavior and set it up to read: **After 3** seconds."

Book Asset Files

Visit this link **www.jamie-cross.net/learnmobilegamedevelopment/assets** to download the source files needed to complete the exercises and games you will create while reading this book.

Thank You Indiegogo Supporters!

Thank you so much to everyone who supported this book on Indiegogo, either through direct contributions or through word of mouth. Your support certainly pushed this book to a higher level!

A special thank you goes out to my Sponsored Backers:
» Jesse Roberts
» Keen*orama Enterprize Pty Ltd.
» Michael James Williams, Tuts+

Dedication

For Brandon: The best son a father could hope for
and my inspiration to try and be better every day.

Chapter 1
Introduction to Game Development with Gamesalad

In This Chapter You Will Learn:

» What game development is

» What Gamesalad is

» How to install Gamesalad

» How to start a new game project

» How to navigate the main Gamesalad interface

This chapter focuses on a discussion about what game development is, what it takes to develop a mobile video game, and how Gamesalad will help you do just that. We will look at the two licenses Gamesalad offers and you will download and install your copy of Gamesalad Creator. Once it's installed, you will learn how to create a new project and begin to set up the basics of a game project, choosing a platform for publishing and setting up a few more initial settings. Finally, you'll take a look at the full Gamesalad interface. This chapter, like this whole book, is intended to be hands-on, so make sure you download and install Gamesalad while reading along.

What is Game Development?

At the simplest level, game development is the process of creating a video game. One person, or a group of people (sometimes up to a hundred or more at a large game studio), can undertake game development. For this book, I will assume you are a single "indie" developer or are working as part of a very small group of two to three people. There are many roles in game development, but as an indie developer, you will likely need to cover several roles all by yourself. Many developers perform all tasks themselves. All game projects will need some combination of game designers, programmers, artists, level designers, sound engineers, and testers. And let's not forget that once the game is complete, someone will need to publish it for the chosen platform(s) and market the game possibly by building a website and contacting the press.

While that sounds like a lot of work, modern game engines, like Gamesalad, really help streamline the entire process.

What is Gamesalad?

Gamesalad Creator is a modern 2D game development kit (GDK). Over 750,000 developers in 189 countries around the world use it and it has been used to make 70 of the top 100 games in the U.S. Apple App Store.

One of the highlights of Gamesalad is that you DO NOT need to learn how to write traditional computer programming code to make your games. Gamesalad offers a simple, yet full-featured, drag and drop interface that lets you build commercial-quality games much quicker than learning traditional programming. Once you are familiar with Gamesalad, you will be able to prototype a game in a few days and complete the entire project in as little as a few weeks instead of the typical months or years it could take to develop a game with another GDK.

Downloading and Installing Gamesalad

For the purpose of this chapter, and the rest of this book, it is assumed you are downloading and using the free Basic version of Gamesalad. If you do purchase the Pro version, you will likely see a few additions to your interface and options, but you can just ignore those while doing the exercises in this book. When you are ready to download Gamesalad, follow these steps:

» Download the Gamesalad installer from the Gamesalad website at http://gamesalad.com/download.
» You'll need to enter an email address and verify that you are at least 13 years of age to download the installer.
» While the software is downloading, you might want to create an account with Gamesalad. This will give you access to Gamesalad's forums, which are a great source of information. Gamesalad staff and many other helpful users support the forums.
» Run the installer and follow the prompts.
» Once the software has finished installing, open the application.

Gamesalad System Requirements

Gamesalad can be run on either a Macintosh or Windows PC computer. Both versions of Gamesalad are able to create the same games; however, the interfaces of the two operating systems are somewhat different. The screen shots in this book are taken from the Macintosh version of Gamesalad. Your computer must meet the minimum system requirements, below, to run Gamesalad.

Macintosh:

» Mac OSX Lion or later. Xcode 4.6 with Command Line Tools and iOS Support. Android SDK for Android support.

» Core 2 Duo or later CPU required. Minimum of 2GB of RAM recommended.

Windows:

» Windows Vista, Windows 7, or Windows 8. Android SDK for Android support.

» Core 2 Duo or Later CPU required. Minimum of 2GB of RAM recommended.

Note: Internet Links

All links to the internet are current and working at the time of this writing. However, URL locations often change. If a link no longer seems correct, a quick Google search will likely lead you to what you are looking for.

Getting to Know Gamesalad Creator

Now that you have Gamesalad Creator installed and running, let's take a look at it and see what it has to offer. Gamesalad Creator is a single piece of software that you will use to bring all of your game's elements together. Sounds, sprites, backgrounds, behaviors, animations, etc. are all assembled in Gamesalad and later published for play on any of the devices that Gamesalad supports. During the publishing process, you will also use Gamesalad's online publishing portal, which we will examine later in this book.

The Splash Screen

The first window you'll see, after opening Gamesalad, is the splash screen (see Figure 1.1). From this splash screen, you can create a new project, open recent projects, and learn more about Gamesalad.

In addition to creating a new project, Gamesalad has several sample projects listed that you can review and learn from. Double-clicking on the project's name (under the create a new project heading) will open any of the sample projects.

As you work on projects in Gamesalad, a menu of past projects will be created under the open recent projects heading. To open any past projects, double-click their name.

The learn section contains links to more detailed instructions located on the Gamesalad website. This section will be great reading once you have completed this book. It will be especially useful if you are looking for more information and are wondering what to do next with your game projects.

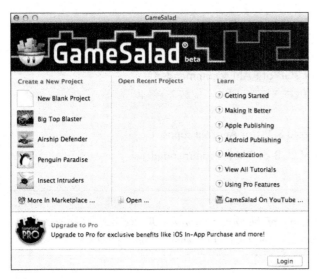

FIGURE 1.1
The Gamesalad splash screen.

Creating a New Project

Let's create your first Gamesalad project! You can either **Double-Click** the new blank project option under the create a new project heading on the splash screen or use the top menu bar and chose **New** from the **File** menu.

Either way, once you have created your first project, you should see a screen like Figure 1.2.

This is the project info screen. The first thing you should do from here is save your new project by going to **Save** from the **File** menu. Make sure you know where you have saved your project so you can find it again next time you want to work on it.

The Project Info Screen

When you start a new project, the first screen that Gamesalad presents to you may initially look overwhelming, but never fear, we are about to fix that! I will give you a quick overview of this collection of buttons and tabs and in the following sections, we'll look at each section in much more detail.

Let's take a look at the fill out boxes and the drop down menu that this screen presents first, from the top down.

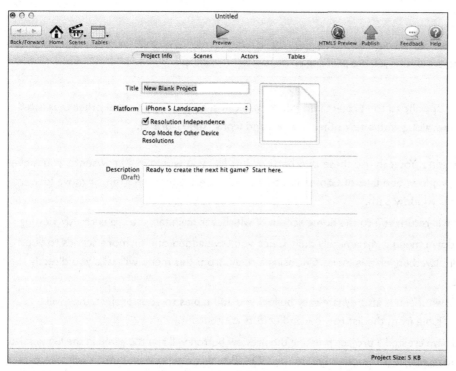

FIGURE 1.2
The Project Info screen.

» **Title:** This should be the name of your game. Typically, you should use the same name that you use when saving your file.

» **Platform:** This drop down menu lists all of the available platforms you can publish to when the game is complete. You should choose the platform you want to develop for BEFORE beginning a project. This choice will set some basic parameters for the project, such as the screen height and width.

» **Resolution Independence:** This check box is only needed (and visible) when you are developing for an Apple iDevice (iPad or iPhone). When you are developing for an iPad or iPhone, you should always make sure you have this option checked. I'll explain why, in more detail, when we discuss graphics and images in another section.

» **Description (Draft):** This area is for your use only and does not affect or get used in the game. You can use this area for notes to yourself, instructions for team members, or leave it empty. It's entirely up to you.

Note: Multiplayer

If you are a Pro-user, you will see an additional drop down menu on this screen. With this menu, you can choose to set up your own multiplayer server if you are planning on developing a multiplayer game.

All of these settings are specific to the project info tab. As you can see, there are several other tabs listed at the top of this window, along with a few other buttons and icons (see Figure 2).

» **Back/Forward Buttons:** You can use these two buttons, just like you would in a browser, as you move through the various windows and tabs of Gamesalad, to go back where you came from, or move forward through your previous window path.

» **Home:** This button will return you to the home screen of whichever main tab you are currently viewing.

» **Scenes:** This drop down menu is dynamically built. Once you have added one or more scenes to your game, they will be displayed under this menu. Choosing a scene from this menu will take you directly to that scenes stage.

» **Tables:** This drop down menu is also dynamically built. If you add tables to your project, they will be listed here. Choose a table from the list to view and edit its contents.

» **Preview:** Once you have created a project, pressing the preview button will run the game in the Gamesalad window, allowing you to play test the game within the GDK. Pressing the preview button will take over the entire Gamesalad screen and hide all other information from view during play testing.

» **HTML5 Preview:** Use this option to preview your game as an HTML5 project. You can preview the game within the Gamesalad environment or within any browser you have installed on your computer.

» **Publish:** Pressing this button will start the app publishing process and you will be directed away from the Gamesalad Creator application to Gamesalad's web-based publishing portal.

» **Feedback and Help:** Pressing either of these buttons will send you to specific help pages, for further assistance, on the Gamesalad website.

» **Project Info Tab:** The project info tab acts as the "home-base" tab of Gamesalad. As you have already seen, this screen is where you establish some initial settings of a project.

» **Scenes Tab:** In this screen, you will add (or delete) new scenes to a game, organize those scenes, and name them.

» **Actors Tab:** From this tab, you can add new actors to a project, delete actors, name actors, and create groups of actors called "tags."

» **Tables Tab:** Just like the other tabs, this tab allows you to add, delete, and name tables within your project.

» **Sign In:** If you are a Pro-user, you'll want to sign into Gamesalad. This will grant you access to the additional features that you have paid for. If you are using the free version, this will make no difference.

» **Project Size:** To give you some idea of how large of a file your final game will be, Gamesalad keeps a running total of your project's final size. This is just an approximation so don't rely on it too much. It's more of a guide than something that is guaranteed.

Note: Scenes, Tables, Actors, and Other Confusing Terms

A lot of this information may seem confusing and overwhelming so early in the book, but never fear! This is just an introduction to the main Gamesalad interface. In the following sections, you'll look at each of these topics, and many more, in great detail. You'll understand them all by the time you have completed all exercises.

Summary

In this chapter, you got your first look at Gamesalad Creator. You downloaded and installed the software on your computer and learned how to open and begin a new game project. You learned how to fill out the requested information in the project info screen and also learned your way around the main Gamesalad interface.

Chapter 2
The Scenes Tab and the Stage

In This Chapter You Will Learn:

» How to add and delete scenes in a game project

» How to organize scenes in a project

» What the stage is and how its used

» How to navigate the stage view

» How to establish some initial settings for a scene

Scenes are one of the base elements that all games are made from in Gamesalad. You will spend this hour learning what a scene is, how and when to add scenes to a project, and how to organize scenes. Once you have learned to add scenes to a project, you'll take a look at the stage view. The stage view is where you will build a scenes' interactive elements and make your game come to life! You'll spend part of this hour learning to navigate the stage view and prepare to add game elements in the next chapter.

The Scenes Tab

The scenes tab is used to create and organize the various scenes of a game. You can think of a scene as an individual level in a game or any single screen of information (like a splash screen, credits screen, etc.). Any time you want to create a new screen, you'll likely do so by creating a new scene in the scenes tab.

The scenes tab opens with one scene already created for you, the initial scene (see Figure 2.1). You can add additional scenes to a project by pressing the **Plus (+)** button in the lower left corner of the screen. As you add new scenes, they will be named and sequentially numbered, starting with scene 1. To rename a scene, click its name and you will be presented with a standard text box to edit. If you add too many scenes to your project, or just want to delete one for any reason, first highlight the scene by clicking on it once. Then you can either press the **Delete** key on your keyboard or press the **Minus (-)** button in the lower left corner of the screen to delete the scene. If you accidently delete a scene, don't worry. Gamesalad has a multi-step undo so you can use the **Edit » Undo** menu option to bring scenes back from nowhere. If you have multiple scenes to delete, you can hold down the **Shift** key, as a modifier, while you are selecting scenes. This will allow you to select multiple scenes at the same time.

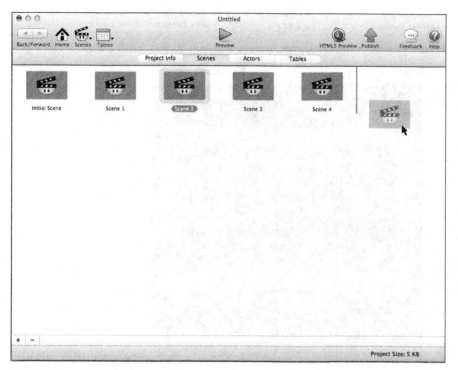

FIGURE 2.1
The Scenes tab.

Once the scenes tab is full of scenes, you will likely want to organize them in a way that makes sense for your project. You can easily move scenes around in the tab by clicking and dragging them to a new location. As you drag a scene, a thin blue line will appear on-screen. When you release the scene, it will move to the location of this blue line and all the other scenes will adjust accordingly.

The Stage View

If you have added scenes to the scenes tab, delete them all except for the default scene named "Initial Scene." **Double-Click** that scene and you'll be presented with the scene's stage view window. You'll see that, again, the screen contents have changed quite a bit (see Figure 2.2). The stage view is the most important screen you will work with; it allows you to see all of the contents of your game. This is where the power of Gamesalad really starts to shine; you don't have to look at line after line of computer programming code to create games. You are able to place all of the game objects on the stage and edit them in real time, allowing you to simply drag and drop your elements to build your games!

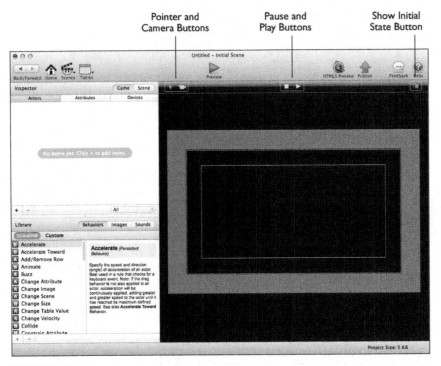

FIGURE 2.2
The Stage view.

Throughout this book, you'll spend a lot of time in the stage view, so let's take a look at all of the new options you have been given. There are three main sections in the stage view window: the inspector palette, the library palette, and the stage itself. Let's take a look at the actual stage first since it is the largest part of the window.

The stage represents the screen size of whichever device you chose for the project's platform on the project info screen. The screen size in Figure 2.2 is the dimensions of the iPhone landscape platform. The stage indicates the live area (in black) of the screen (this is the area that you will see on-screen while playing the game) and also a gray area that acts as a pasteboard while working on a project. The white lines are indications of some camera settings. The outside line is the area the camera "sees" and the inside line indicates the camera's movement leeway zone. Later in the book, we'll look at the camera settings in more detail.

There are a few new buttons placed across the top of the stage as well; all of these buttons turn blue when they are active.

» **Pointer Button:** Returns you to stage-editing mode if you are in camera-editing mode.

» **Camera Button:** Sends you into camera-editing mode from stage-editing mode. When in camera-editing mode, you can use the on-screen handles to adjust the camera's movement leeway zone.

» **Pause Button:** Pressing the pause button will pause the gameplay.

» **Play Button:** Pressing the play button will run the game on the stage, leaving all other tabs and information on the screen. This is different from the large green preview button above that hides all extraneous information while play testing the game.

» **Show Initial State Button:** When this button is active, any moving elements in the game will leave a "shadow" image at their initial location. This can be helpful when play testing; you can tell where an actor has moved to and from, that way you can make adjustments as needed. You can toggle this button on and off while the game is running.

The Inspector Palette

This palette can be separated into two tabs, the game and scene tabs, each of which have subsections of information.

Game Tab

The game tab is separated into three subsections: actors, attributes, and devices (see Figure 2.3).

» **Actors:** An actor is any object that will be used in a game; it could be a sprite, a piece of text, a special effect, etc.

» **Attributes:** An attribute is what Gamesalad calls a variable. Gamesalad has many built-in attributes and you can also add your own as needed. Attributes can hold numerical or text data.

» **Devices:** Contains a list of various device-related attributes that can be accessed during gameplay.

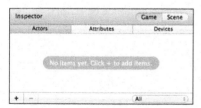

FIGURE 2.3
The Game tab in the Inspector Palette.

Scene Tab

The scene tab has two subsections of information: attributes and layers (see Figure 2.4).

» **Attributes:** This is a listing of scene-specific attributes that can be edited to customize each scene of your game.

» **Layers:** The layers tab lets you create multiple layers of actors in a scene to help visually organize your games.

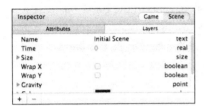

FIGURE 2.4
The Scene tab in the Inspector Palette.

The Library Palette

This palette is separated into three tabs: behaviors, images, and sounds. And just like the inspector palette, each of these tabs has their own subset of additional information.

Behaviors Tab

Behaviors are Gamesalad's preset blocks of "code" that you will drag and drop onto actors to build a game's interactivity. There is a pre-made behavior for just about any action you can imagine. If one does not already exist by the end of this book, you'll be able to customize your own to fit your needs. Behaviors are further separated into two subcategories: standard and custom (see Figure 2.5).

» **Standard:** Standard behaviors are all of the behaviors that ship with the free Gamesalad license.

» **Custom:** This is a customizable area that you can use to store your own custom-built behaviors.

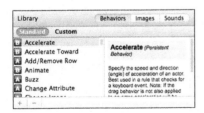

FIGURE 2.5
The Behaviors tab in the Library Palette.

Note: Pro Behaviors

If you purchased the Pro license for Gamesalad, you will see a third group called "Pro." Pro behaviors offer some additional features like including advertising in a game, linking a game to Twitter, opening URL's within a game, and more.

Images Tab

The images tab is used to store all of the images that have been imported into a project. The images tab is further separated into project and purchased (see Figure 2.6). At the bottom of the window is a slider control that can be used to increase and decrease the size of the icon preview of images that are displayed in the window.

» **Project:** Displays images imported into the current project.

» **Purchase:** Displays images purchased from the Gamesalad marketplace.

FIGURE 2.6
The Images tab in the Library Palette.

Sounds Tab

The sounds tab is used to store all of the audio files that have been imported into a project. The Sounds tab is further separated into project and purchased (see Figure 2.7).

» **Project:** Displays audio files imported into the current project.

» **Purchase:** Displays audio file purchased from the Gamesalad marketplace.

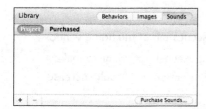

FIGURE 2.7
The Sounds tab in the Library Palette.

Tip: Organizing Your Projects

While Gamesalad helps you organize your project with these palettes, it's also a good idea to set up a specific directory structure on your computer for each project you are working on. As you learn more and your projects get larger, all of the files can quickly get out of hand. Figure 2.8 is a screen shot of how I like to set up my file structure. As you can see there is a specific folder location for each kind of file that might be used in a game.

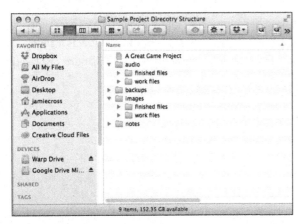

FIGURE 2.8
Sample directory structure with file locations clearly named.

Scene Inspector Details

Before we finish this chapter, let's return to the scene tab of the inspector palette. As I briefly mentioned above, this section is used to customize each scene within a game. If you have a game with ten different scenes, each scene can have different settings in their own scene tab (these are scene-specific settings not game-specific). The scene attributes tab (see Figure 2.9) contains a few options you are likely to edit often, some of which include:

» **Name:** This is the name of the scene and can also be edited in the scenes tab of the home window.

» **Size, Width, and Height:** This is the pixel dimension of the current scene. If you want to make a scene that is larger than the device, so your game can scroll in some direction, you would increase the size of the scene here.

» **Wrap X:** When wrap x is active, an actor that leaves the stage on the right side of the screen will wrap around to the left side and reappear there. If an actor leaves on the left side, it will reappear on the right side.

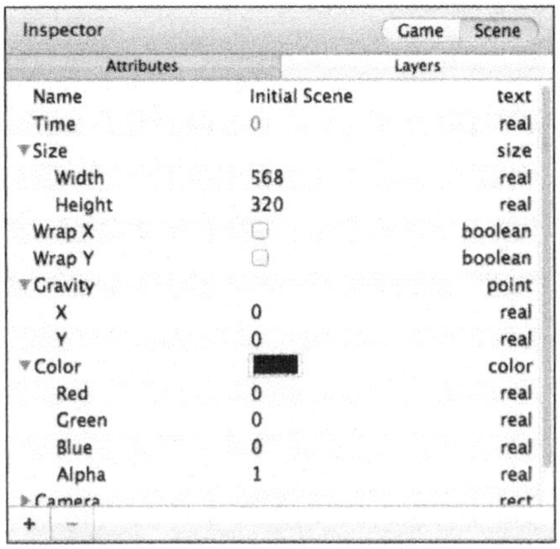

Inspector		Game	Scene
Attributes		Layers	
Name	Initial Scene		text
Time	0		real
▼Size			size
Width	568		real
Height	320		real
Wrap X	☐		boolean
Wrap Y	☐		boolean
▼Gravity			point
X	0		real
Y	0		real
▼Color	▓▓▓▓		color
Red	0		real
Green	0		real
Blue	0		real
Alpha	1		real
▸Camera			rect

FIGURE 2.9
Details of the Scenes tab in the Inspector Palette.

» **Wrap Y:** When wrap y is active, an actor that leaves the stage on the top of the screen will wrap around to the bottom and reappear there. If an actor leaves from the bottom, it will reappear on the top of the screen.

» **Gravity, X, and Y:** You can apply gravity to a scene with these attributes. Gravity does not have to always move an object from the top of the play area to the bottom; you can adjust these values to make objects "fall up" the screen if you want too!

» **Color, Red, Green, and Blue:** You can adjust the background color of the scene by clicking on the color swatch provided and by picking a color from the color picker or you can manually adjust the values of red, green, and blue.

Summary

In this chapter, you learned all about the scenes tab and how to add and organize scenes. You learned about the stage view, what its various parts are, and how to navigate through the palettes. Lastly, you learned how to establish some initial settings for each scene so you can have a lot of variety in your games.

Chapter 3

Game Objects and Gamesalad's Coordinate System

In This Chapter You Will Learn:

» How the Gamesalad coordinate system works

» How to add a new game actor to a project

» How to work with actors

In Gamesald, every single object used in a game is called an "actor." The stage and every actor placed on it have a set of coordinates that are used to place and control them. In this chapter, you will learn all about the coordinate systems of the stage and its actors. You'll finish off the chapter by placing an actor on the stage and by learning the different ways you can manipulate that actor to control its precise appearance and placement.

Coordinates and Dimensions

When you are playing a video game, it may seem like all of the objects on the screen are placed in random locations, but in reality, the computer numerically placed them on-screen using a system of dimensions and coordinates. While you are playing the game, the computer keeps track of every on-screen element and knows exactly where they are at all times using these same systems. Gamesalad is a 2D game engine, so all of its coordinate systems are two-dimensional as well.

Note: 2D vs. 3D

Gamesalad uses a two-dimensional (2D) system to create and control all of its games. The 2D system is a flat system that deals with only horizontal and vertical elements. Three-dimensional (3D) systems deal with the same horizontal and vertical elements, but add depth as an additional element.

The Coordinate System

The coordinate system used by Gamesalad (and most other game engines) is a series of lines (called axes) and locations (called points). These axes and points allow every object in the game to be precisely placed and manipulated as needed. The 2D coordinate system has an x-axis and a y-axis. These axes represent the horizontal (x) and vertical (y) directions. When an object moves vertically, it is said to be moving along the y-axis. However, when an object moves horizontally, it is said to be moving along the x-axis. Figure 3.1 shows a typical 2D coordinate system.

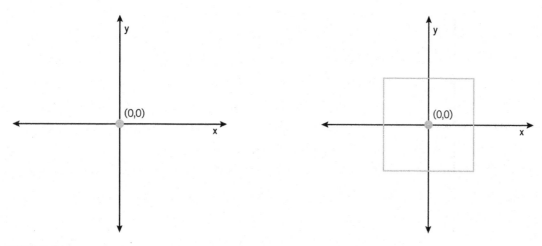

FIGURE 3.1
2D coordinate system.

As you can see in the figure above, the coordinate system has a point where the x- and y-axis meet. This point is known as the origin. The coordinates for the origin of a 2D coordinate system are always 0 on the x-axis and 0 on the y-axis.

Note: Writing Coordinates

Referring to coordinates, like I just did above, is rather long-winded and can quickly become old. It is commonly accepted to write a set of coordinates as (x,y). So, the origin of a coordinate system would be written as (0,0).

The origin of the coordinate system is important because it is the location by which all other points are determined. The coordinates for all other points are simply the distance of that point from the origin, along the correct axis. Gamesalad measures distance between points as pixels or fractions of a pixel. A point's coordinate will get larger as it moves further away from the origin. For example, as a point moves up, its y-axis value will get larger. If that same point moves down, the y-axis gets smaller. If that point passes through the origin, it will become a negative value and begin to increase as it again moves further away from the origin. Figure 3.2 has four points plotted the origin at (0,0) and three other points. The point at

(2,4) is 2 units to the right of the origin and 4 units above the origin. The point plotted at (3,-2) is 3 points to the right of the origin and two points below. And the final point plotted at (-3,-3) is 3 points to the left and 3 points below the origin.

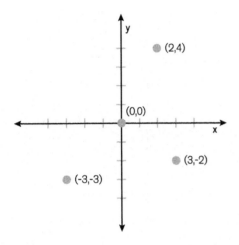

FIGURE 3.2
2D coordinate system, with plotted points.

The Coordinate System of the Stage and its Actors

The stage in Gamesalad uses a coordinate system to place and manage all of the actors and elements you will place on-screen while you are building and testing a project. The origin of the stage in Gamesalad is in the lower left corner of the screen (see Figure 3.3).

As you can see, by placing a coordinate system over the stage, the origin is in the bottom left corner. The points on the coordinate system will extend to the right and above the origin until you reach the limits of the scene's size. For an iPhone 5 in landscape orientation, the furthest points visible on-screen will be 568 pixels to the right and 320 pixels above the origin. If an object moves to a negative value below or to the left of the stage, or to a positive value to the right or above the origin that is greater than the scene size, it will disappear off the screen.

In addition to the coordinate system used for the stage, each actor has its own local coordinate system (see Figure 3.4).

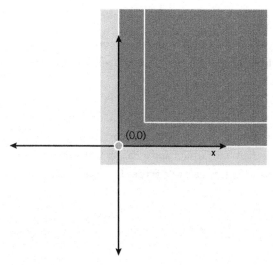

FIGURE 3.3
Plotted origin of the Stages coordinate system.

The stage's coordinate system, on the left, represents a square actor placed on the stage. The four corners of the square are plotted from the origin of the stage. The actor's coordinate system is shown on the right, with the origin of the actor as its center and the four corners of the actor plotted from its own origin. In the next section, you'll see why it is important to keep the stage and actor's coordinate systems in mind as you create your projects.

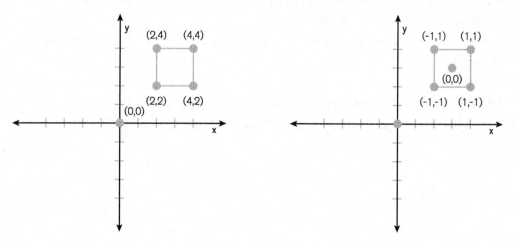

FIGURE 3.4
(Left) points plotted from the origin of the stage, (right) points plotted from the actors origin.

Actors (Game Objects)

In Gamesalad, every object you place on the stage (such as sprites, text, backgrounds, sounds, etc.) are all considered actors. Anytime you want to place a new object of any kind in a game, you will need to create a new actor to do it.

When you create a new actor, it is really nothing more than an empty square box with a collection of attributes associated with it. The magic of Gamesalad is that by adding images, behaviors, and custom attributes to these actors, you can quickly and easily turn them into useful and amazing elements in your game. A large part of this book will be spent learning how to create amazing actors for your projects.

Exercise 1

Create Your First Actor

In this exercise, you'll create an actor, place it on the stage, and examine its initial settings.

1. Open Gamesalad and create a new blank project.
2. For the Platform, choose iPad Landscape. This will give you a nice, big area to experiment with.
3. **Click** the Scenes tab and **Double-Click** the Initial Scene to go to its Stage.
4. In the Actors tab of the Inspector palette, **Click** the **Plus (+)** button in the lower left corner to add a new Actor to the project.
5. Actor 1 is automatically named and added to the list of actors.
6. **Double-Click** Actor 1 and you'll see that Gamesalad gives every actor a basic set of components (Attributes) that define the Actor.
7. Don't worry about making any changes to these at this moment; we'll take a detailed look at all this information later in the book.
8. **Click** the **Back** button to return to the Stage.
9. **Drag** Actor 1, from the Actors tab, onto the black area of the Stage and let it go.
10. Congratulations, you have just created and placed your first actor in Gamesalad!

Fine-Tuning Actors on the Stage

Now that you have your first actor placed on the stage, let's take a few minutes and look at the various ways you can control its placement and appearance so you can make your games exactly like you imagine them.

Movement

Once you have placed an actor on the stage, it has a plotted location on the coordinate system of the stage. When you move an actor on the stage, you are changing its plotted position. You can move actors along the x-axis, the y-axis, or some combination of both. Moving along both axis results in a diagonal line of movement. To move an actor on the stage, click it once and drag it to a new location.

Select the square Actor you placed on the Stage in the previous exercise by clicking it once. When clicked, you'll see that a set of lines and circles appear around the actor's edge. This indicates that an actor is "active" and also acts as a set of controls for moving and adjusting the actor (see Figure 3.5).

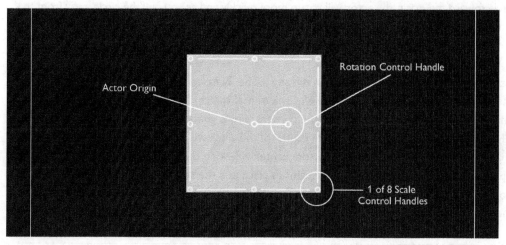

FIGURE 3.5
An active actor displaying its control handles.

The open circle in the direct center of the actor represents its local origin. To move an actor, click on it and drag it to a new location. Make sure you DO NOT click on any of the highlights, circles, or lines, or else you may accidently rotate or resize the actor. Move the Actor so its center circle is overlapping the red plus sign in the center of the Stage. When you move the Actor, you are really just moving its center point of origin.

NOTE: Actor Controls

All adjustments (movement, rotation, and scaling) made to actors take place from their local origin (its center point).

You can also move an actor by pressing the arrow keys on the keyboard. With the Actor still highlighted, press the **Right Arrow** key a few times. Each press of the arrow key moves the actor along its axis, one pixel at a time. This is great for pixel perfect adjustments.

Rotation

To rotate an actor, click it once to activate it and note the white line and circle that extends out of the actor's center. This acts as a rotation control for the actor. After clicking on the circle at the end of the line (not the origin), you can drag that circle around the origin to rotate the actor (see Figure 3.5 above).

As you drag the circle around the origin, you can also move the circle into or away from the origin. As you move the circle toward the origin, the actor will rotate more quickly and as you pull the circle away from the origin, the actor will rotate more slowly. When you are finished rotating the actor, release the rotation control.

Scaling

Scaling an actor will make it larger or smaller on the stage. The 8 circles located around the edge of the actor are the scale controls (see Figure 3.5 above). Click one of the circles and drag the actor to make it larger or smaller. Selecting one of the circles at the corners allows you to scale the actor both horizontally and vertically at the same time. The circles in the center of the sides will only scale the actor horizontally and the remaining two circles in the top and bottom center will scale the actor vertically. When scaling an actor, the opposite side from where you click remains in place and the rest of the actor changes size. However, note that the origin moves as the actor scales. Remember, the origin is always located at the center of the actor.

TIP: Modifier Keys

*When adjusting an actor's placement on the stage, you are able to use the **Shift** and **Option (Alt)** keys as modifiers to certain actions.*

The Shift Key

» *When moving an actor, hold down the **Shift** key to limit its movement to only the x- and y-axis.*

» *Hold down the **Shift** key during rotation to limit the actor's rotation to 45° increments.*

» *Use the **Shift** key when scaling an actor from its corner point to scale proportionally in that direction.*

The Option (Alt) Key

» *Holding down the **Option (Alt)** key while moving an actor will make a copy of that actor.*

» *When scaling an actor using a corner point, holding down the **Option (Alt)** key will scale the actor in all four directions at once.*

» *Holding down the **Option (Alt)** key while scaling an actor using a side point will scale the actor equally in both directions along that axis.*

Adjusting the actor's attributes gives you even more precise control over all of these settings, rotation, scaling, and movement. We'll look at that, in much more detail, later in the book.

Summary

In this chapter, you learned all about the coordinate system of the stage and the local coordinate system of actors. You learned how these coordinates are used to place and control all of your game's elements. You then created and placed an actor on the stage and learned the various ways to control, place, and size that actor.

Chapter 4
Actors and Their Attributes

In This Chapter You Will Learn:

» How to customize actors in your game

» The difference between a prototype and an instance actor

» What actor attributes are and how to use some of them

In this chapter, you'll learn more details about actors in Gamesalad. You'll learn how to begin customizing actors with your own images (sprites). Then you will go hands-on with learning the difference between a prototype and an instance actor. Finally, you will learn about the extensive list of attributes each actor is given and learn how to add your own custom attributes as well.

Actors in Detail

In the last chapter, you learned a little bit about actors. In this hour, you'll keep going and learn more details about actors and why they are so important to your games. As mentioned in the last chapter, any item placed on the stage in Gamesalad is called an actor–these can be static (non-animated) sprites, animated sprites, sounds, and even text. As you have seen, Gamesalad's default actor is a white square, which is not the most exciting element to work with in the world! But the great thing is you can endlessly customize this basic actor to meet all your game creation needs.

Importing Images

The easiest way to customize your actor is to replace the basic white square with an exciting and beautiful image. Gamesalad supports the PNG image file format. This format allows you to have full-color images with an alpha channel for transparency. In a later chapter, we will take an in-depth look at image formats and requirements.

Exercise 2

Importing an Image to Customize the Actor.

In this exercise, you will import your own image for use as an actor in Gamesalad.

1. Create a new iPhone 5 Landscape Project in Gamesalad. Make sure you have checked the Resolution Independence option on the Project Info tab.

2. Navigate to the empty Initial Scene and **Click** the Images tab in the Library Palette (see Figure 4.1).

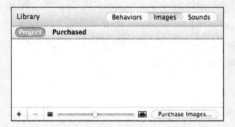

FIGURE 4.1
The Images Tab in
the Library Palette

3. **Click** the **Plus (+)** button, in the lower left corner of this tab, and use the Open Dialog Box that appears to locate the file named "Ball.png" provided for you in the Chapter 4 folder of the book asset files.

4. Once the Ball.png file has been added to the project, you'll see an icon and the file name now listed in the Images tab.

5. Next, make sure the Actors tab is active in the Inspector Palette above the Library Palette and **Click** the **Plus (+)** button to add a new, empty Actor to the project.

6. Finally, **Drag** the ball image from the Images tab and drop it onto Actor 1.

7. Actor 1 will highlight (see Figure 4.2) when the ball image is touching it. When you release the Mouse button, Actor 1 will now look like a ball!

8. Save this project for use later in this chapter.

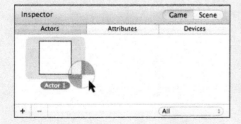

FIGURE 4.2
Actor 1 highlights to indicate the
image will be applied when the
mouse button is released.

NOTE: Other Ways to Make an Actor

Once you have imported an image, there are a couple "quick" ways to turn it into an actor. You can drag the image directly from the images tab and drop it in the actors tab or onto the stage (Gamesalad will automatically create a new actor using the same name as the image).

The Gamesalad Marketplace

If you can't draw to save your life, and you don't have any artist friends, you may find the Gamesalad Marketplace helpful. In the bottom right corner of the images tab, there is a button labeled "Purchase Images." Pressing this button will direct you to the Gamesalad Marketplace in your systems default browser. From here, you are able to purchase images, sounds, animations, and full game templates. This can be a valuable resource for those who are artistically or time challenged.

Actor Types: Prototype and Instance

There are two types of actors in Gamesalad: prototype and instance. When an actor is first created in the actors tab, it is created as a prototype actor. You can confirm this by double-clicking the actor to open its actor editor. **Double-Click** the new ball actor "Actor 1" you created in the previous exercise. At the top of the window, next to the actor's name it says "Prototype" (see Figure 4.3). A prototype actor is a "master" actor. Any changes made to a prototype actor are applied to all other actors of that type in the game.

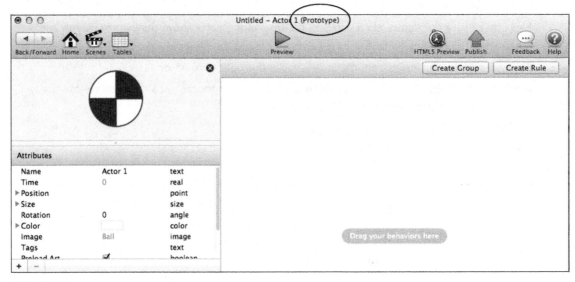

FIGURE 4.3
The title of the Actor Editor indicating that this actor is a Prototype Actor.

To create an instance of an actor, drag the ball actor "Actor 1" onto the Stage and **Double-Click** it. The Actor Editor will open up, but this time there is a large padlock icon on-screen that says "Click the lock to edit the behaviors of this actor" (see Figure 4.4). When the padlock icon is clicked it will disappear and there will be an active button in the top left area of the screen that says "Revert to Prototype." This button indicates you are looking at the actor editor of an instance actor.

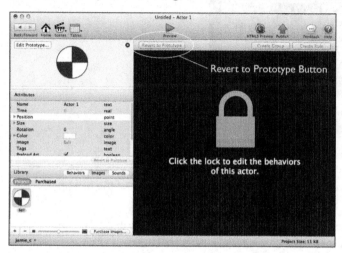

FIGURE 4.4
The padlock icon of an Instance Actor.

Let's take a look at the differences between a prototype and instance of the same actor.

Exercise 3

Using Prototype and Instance Actors

If you were going to use the ball actor to make an 8-Ball Pool game, you would need 15 balls in the game. While all of the balls in a pool game should be the same size, they should all be different colors. Let's see how you can accomplish this with just one actor.

1. Using the "ball" project you have been working on, return to the Stage and delete any elements currently on it.
2. **Single Click** on the name of Actor 1 and change the name to "Ball".
3. Drag two copies of the ball actor onto the Stage; place one on the left and one on the right so they don't overlap each other (see Figure 4.5).

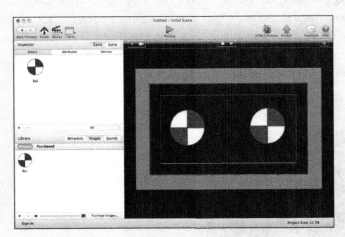

FIGURE 4.5
Two copies of the ball actor
placed on the stage.

4. To reduce the size of both balls at once, **Double-Click** the Prototype actor of the ball (in the Actors tab of the Inspector palette).

5. In the Attributes section of this screen, **Click** the arrow next to the Size Attribute. This will expose the Width and Height Attributes.

6. Reduce the current value of 128 to 64 for both Width and Height (see Figure 4.6).

Attributes		
Name	Ball	text
Time	0	real
▶ Position		point
▼ Size		size
Width	128	real
Height	128	real
Rotation	0	angle
▶ Color		color
Image	Ball	image
+ −		

FIGURE 4.6
The actors size settings
in the Attributes tab.

7. **Click** the **Back** button to return to the Stage and you'll see that the size of BOTH ball actors has been changed.

8. Next, to change the color of only the ball on the right, **Double-Click** it and **Click** the Lock icon to unlock the instance.

9. Again, in the Attributes section of this actor, **Click** the white rectangle next to the Color option (see Figure 4.7).

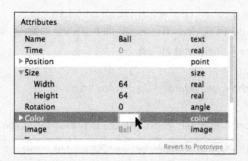

FIGURE 4.7
The actors Color choice
in the Attributes tab.

10. From the standard color wheel that pops up on-screen, choose a nice, bright yellow color.

11. Return to the Stage and you'll see that ONLY the actor on the right has changed color!

As you can see, edits made to a prototype actor affect all actors of that type while edits made to the instance of an actor only affect that individual instance.

Actor Attributes

Every actor in Gamesalad starts with an extensive list of attributes that can be used to control everything from its appearance, to its position on the stage, and even its physical properties within a game (see Figure 4.8). The list may look long and daunting, but by the end of this chapter, you'll have a good understanding of it.

Attributes		
Name	Ball	text
Time	0	real
▼ Position		point
X	0	real
Y	0	real
▼ Size		size
Width	64	real
Height	64	real
Rotation	0	angle
▼ Color		color
Red	1	real
Green	1	real
Blue	1	real
Alpha	1	real
Image	Ball	image
Tags		text
Preload Art	☑	boolean
▼ Graphics		attributes
Visible	☑	boolean
Blending Mode	Normal	enumeration
Horizontal Wrap	Stretch	enumeration
Vertical Wrap	Stretch	enumeration

FIGURE 4.8
A portion of an actors
Attributes tab.

The actor attributes tab is separated into three columns: the first column is the name of the attribute, the second column is the attribute's initial value, and the third column is the attribute's type. Later in this book, we'll spend another hour looking at attributes in detail. In that chapter, you'll learn the differences between the six attribute types (boolean, text, integer, real, angle, and index).

Starting from the top of the list, let's examine some of the most typically used actor attributes:

» **Position X:** This is the actor's position on the x- (horizontal) axis. Positions are expressed in pixels.

» **Position Y:** This is the actor's position on the y- (vertical) axis. Positions are expressed in pixels.

» **Size-Width:** This is the width of the actor on the stage. This is expressed in pixels.

» **Size-Height:** This is the height of the actor on the stage. This is expressed in pixels.

» **Rotation:** This is the rotation of the actor. It is expressed in degrees and can vary from 0° to 359°.

» **Color:** You can choose a color from the standard system color picker by clicking the rectangular color box or you can manually set the values by adjusting the red, green, blue, and alpha values of the color. The numeric values for the color attributes can vary between 0 and 1.

» **Tags:** Tags are used to "group" actors into sets so actions can be performed on them all at once. You'll explore this more in a future chapter. Tags are entered as a text value.

» **Graphics-Visible:** If this box is checked (active), the actor will be visible when placed on the stage. An unchecked setting means the actor will not be visible.

» **Graphics-Horizontal and Vertical Wrap:** These Attributes affect your actor when it is re-sized. There are three options in the drop-down menus:

> » **Stretch:** This will scale the actor's image up or down as the actor is scaled.

> » **Fixed:** This will keep the actor's image sized to its real pixel dimensions, even as the actor is scaled.

> » **Tile:** This will repeat the actor's image as needed when the actors size is increased on stage. This option is great for making repeating textures, tiles or shapes.

Let's look at the three graphics wrapping settings in action. In Figures 4.9A-C below, the "original" actor is always on the left and the actor that has been scaled is on the right. In Figure 4.9A, the ball's image has stretched to fill the new actor's size completely. In Figure 4.9B, the ball's image has remained at the source images size, even while the actor itself has increased (note the actor's control/guide lines around the small ball). And in Figure 4.9C, the ball has repeated to fill the larger actor's size.

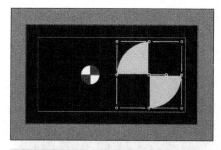

FIGURE 4.9A
The actor on the right has been enlarged using the Stretch option of the Horizontal/Verticle Wrap menu.

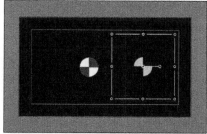

FIGURE 4.9B
The actor on the right has been enlarged using the Fixed option of the Horizontal/Verticle Wrap menu.

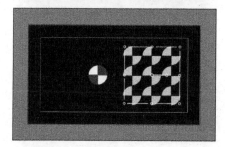

FIGURE 4.9C
The actor on the right has been enlarged using the Tile option of the Horizontal/Verticle Wrap menu.

» **Graphics-Flip Horizontally and Flip Vertically:** These attributes will flip an actor's image along its x- or y-axis. These are extremely helpful when animating an actor. Using these setting you can create an animation for one direction and flip it when you need your actor to move in the opposite direction instead of creating two full sets of animated images.

NOTE: Alpha

I have mentioned the term "Alpha" several times during the first four chapters. Alpha (also know as alpha channel) represents the level of transparency of an image. Usually, it is expressed as a number value from 0 (fully transparent) to 1 (opaque/solid). It can also be expressed as values of black in an image-processing program like Adobe Photoshop where black is transparent and white is opaque.

There are many more actor attributes that you have access to, including a whole host of physics settings that we will take a look at in a future chapter. These may seem like a lot to take in, but once you've become more familiar with actors and their attributes, you'll be surprised by how quickly you become familiar with them all.

In addition to the built-in list of actor attributes, you are able to add your own custom attributes as well. You can add and delete your own attributes to and from the list by using the plus (+) and minus (-) buttons in the lower left corner of the actors attributes tab. We'll discuss how and why you'd want to add your own attributes in a later hour.

Summary

In this chapter, you learned how to begin to customize the actors in a game by adding custom images to them. You learned the important difference between a prototype and instance actors and how and when to create each type. Finally, you learned about some of the many attributes each actor has and what those attributes can be used for.

Chapter 5
Game 1–Pachinko/Plinko

In This Chapter You Will Learn:

» How to design a simple game

» How to apply your knowledge of the stage and actors

» How to add interactive elements to the game

» The importance of play testing the finished game

In this chapter, you will take what you have learned so far and apply it to your first full game using Gamesalad. We will start by discussing game design/planning and how it applies to this game. Afterwards, you will build the environment for the game, build and add the actors to this environment and finally play test the game.

What is Game Design?

Put simply, the design phase of a video game is the act of planning the rules, content, gameplay, environments, storyline, etc. of the game ahead of time. Not every game will cover all of those elements. For example, the game you are about to create will not have any storyline since it's an arcade game. During this phase, the planning of the project is often done on paper, with flow charts for interactions, level designs drawn up, characters illustrated, and even coding rules roughed out. Since this game is very straightforward with one screen and ten Actors, you won't need to do all of that detailed pre-planning. But keep in mind, as your projects grow in size and detail, the more up-front planning you can do, the easier the project will flow. For this game project, we are going to plan the gameplay, the asset requirements, and the rules of the game.

The Gameplay

For your first game, you are going to create a simple version of Pachinko. Pachinko is
style game. A ball is dropped through a field of pegs, falling down the screen to a gro
the bottom of the screen. This game will be easy to assemble with the knowledge yc
teach some new and important concepts as well.

The Asset Requirements

An asset is any object that will be needed to produce the final game. It can be an art element, a sound file, or a piece of text. Often times, a large group of people work on a video game—many people may work on completing the different assets at the same time. But, as I mentioned in the beginning of this book, it's likely you are either a solo developer or part of a very small team, so you may be creating every asset in your games yourself. All of the assets for Pachinko are already created for you and included in a starter project.

NOTE: Starter and Complete Project

The starter project for Pachinko is located in the book assets for Chapter 5. This starter project contains some of the elements you'll need to complete this chapter's work. If you get stuck building the game, or things don't seem to be working correctly, there is also a fully-completed project in the book assets for Chapter 5 that you can use for reference.

Below is a list of the assets that are required for Pachinko:

» A game board. This board will be a single scene in Gamesalad.

» Art for the ball, pegs, wood planks, and background. This art is provided for you in the starter project.

» Actors for the ball, pegs, wood planks, and background. These are part of the starter project.

» A game control actor. This is part of the starter project.

The Rules of the Game

Whether it's a board game, a sports game, or a video game, every game must have rules. The game's rules let the players know how to play the game and also let you, as the game's developer, know how to create the game. Once you have planned your game's rules, you can use that plan to code the rules and behaviors in Gamesalad (or any other programming language you choose).

TIP: Coding

Whatever you choose to call it—coding, scripting, or programming—it is the act of telling a computer how to interpret events in a game. If you don't specifically tell the computer what to do when an event occurs in your game, nothing will happen when that event occurs. For example, if you don't tell the computer what to do when the ball hits a peg in this Pachinko game, the ball will just pass through the peg as if it wasn't there.

The rules of Pachinko are below:

» The ball will start at the top of the screen and continuously move side to side until the player clicks the mouse button.

» When the mouse button is clicked, the ball will drop down the screen.

» When the ball collides with a peg or a board, the ball will bounce.

» A bounce sound will play whenever the ball bounces off of a peg or board.

As you can see, by reading through the rules, each one relates to the previous and they cover every action possible in the game. As your games get more complex, it may be beneficial to create a flow chart of rules to show how they relate to each other.

NOTE: Definitions

Game development contains a lot of specialized terms; a few are mentioned in the sections above:

» *Game Controller: A game controller is a special actor in a game that "watches" for certain events to happen and triggers other events at the correct times. A game controller can be any actor in the game—often it is a special actor that is created specifically for this purpose and is placed on the pasteboard in Gamesalad.*

» *Collide: Colliding is a term used to describe when two or more objects touch each other during a game.*

» *Spawn: Spawning is when a new actor is added to the stage during a game.*

Creating the Game

With all of the pre-planning complete, it's time to start building the actual, working game. Since this is your first game project, there is a starter project named "Pachinko-Starter" located in the book assets for chapter 5. Some of the elements are already built for you. However, there is a lot of work remaining to be done. When you have completed the project, it should look like Figure 5.1.

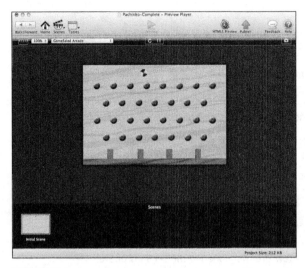

FIGURE 5.1
The completed Pachinko game.

Open the Starter File

Open the file named "Pachinko-Starter." Before you start building the game, note that this game is set up for the Gamesalad Arcade Platform type. Remember that you can check this in the project info tab. Go to the Scenes tab and **Double-Click** the Initial Scene to go to its Stage. At this point, you should see an empty stage on the right and five blank/empty actors in the actors tab of the inspector palette.

Completing the Actors

First, you must import the images you'll need for the actors so you can build the game board that all of the action will take place on. These images are provided for you in the images folder located in the assets for chapter 5 folder.

1.   **Click** on the Images tab in the Library Palette.
2.   **Click** the **Plus (+)** button and navigate to the Images folder for chapter 5.
3.   Import the images named "background-guide.png," "ball.png," "board.png," and "peg.png."

NOTE: Group Selecting

*In the open dialog box, you can hold down the **Command** key on your keyboard and select all four of the images at the same time (that way you don't have to import them one at a time).*

---

4.   Next, drag the images to each of the Actors of the same name. The image named "background-guide" should be dragged onto the Actor named "background.", etc.

Make sure to drag these images ONTO the actors provided. DO NOT create new actors with them. The Actors tab should now look like Figure 5.2. Some of the actors provided for you already have behaviors applied to them; these behaviors are going to make the game work properly.

Note: Behaviors

In this chapter, you will be adding one of the behaviors yourself, but since you have not learned about behaviors yet, I have provided you with the others needed to complete this game.

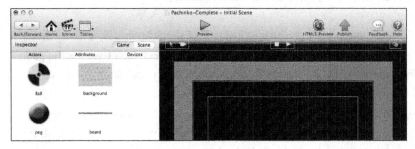

FIGURE 5.2
The Actors Tab with images applied to each actor.

Building the Game Board

Now that you have completed the actors by adding their images, you should build the game board next.

1.   First, drag the Actor named "background" and place its origin point so it is over the red plus at the center of the Stage.
2.   **Double-Click** the background Actor that you just placed on Stage. In its Attributes editor, change Position x to 240 and Position y to 160 (this is the exact center of the Stage).

Note: Center Stage

The coordinates of the stage's center depend on the scene size. Because the Gamesalad Arcade Platform is 480 x 320 pixels, the center of that stage is (240,160). You can calculate the center of the stage by dividing each of its dimensions by 2. If the platform was something different, the center point of the stage would be different as well.

With the background actor placed, the next thing to do is place all of the pegs on-screen. As you can see, the background actor has four lines of gray circles placed on it. These circles are guides indicating where to place all of the peg actors. Take a couple minutes and drag 30 peg actors onto the Stage, placing them on top of each gray circle (see Figure 5.1 above).

Note: Peg Placement

It's not critical to cover each circle with the pegs you place. The circles are only there as a guide. Remember, if you want to do small adjustments to an actor's placement, you can nudge them one pixel at a time using the arrow keys on the keyboard.

Finally, you'll place the boards on-screen and the game board will be complete.

1. **Drag** a copy of the "board" Actor and place it at the very bottom of the Stage.
2. **Double-Click** this board and make its Position (240,10). This board will act as the base for the game board when the ball falls from the top of the screen. This board will stop the ball from completely falling off the bottom of the screen.
3. Next, you'll add the four divider boards that will make up the score cups. Drag a new board actor onto the Stage and release it anywhere. **Single Click** the board to highlight it. Once highlighted, use the board's rotation handle (while holding down the **Shift** key) to rotate the board 90°.
4. Now, **Double-Click** this board and change its Position to (91,-190).
5. Return to the Stage and highlight this new board. Make a copy of it by holding down the **Option** key and dragging the new copy slightly to the right. Change its Position to (192,-190).
6. Make two more copies of this board and set their Positions as (289,-190) and (385,-190).

Now, you'll need to adjust the layer order of these boards. In the Inspector palette, **Click** the Scene button and then **Click** the Layers tab. **Click** the Arrow icon next to the layer named "Background". This will open the background layers' contents, showing you every actor that is placed on the stage so far in the game. Like most layer systems in other software packages, the top item on the list is above all the other items below it on stage. You'll need to drag the first board placed, to the very top of this list, so it looks like a continuous floor across the bottom of the screen. Grab the fifth board from the top of this list and drag it to the top position. Once you have placed the bottom board at the top of the list, **Click** on the gray pasteboard of the Stage to deactivate any active actors. Your screen should look like Figure 5.3.

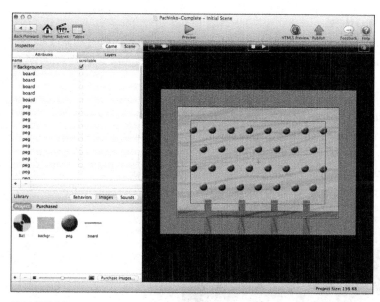

FIGURE 5.3
The Layers Palette showing the contents of the Background layer.

To complete the game board, return to the Actors tab and drag two more copies of the board Actor onto the screen and rotate each one 90°. On the Pasteboard, place one directly to the left of the Stage and the other directly to the right of the Stage. These boards will not show on-screen during gameplay, but they will act as walls to keep the ball from falling off the edge of the play area. The game board is now complete and should look like Figure 5.4.

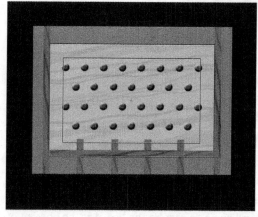

FIGURE 5.4
The completed game board with all 30 pegs and 7 boards in place.

Adding the Game Controller

Now that you have completed the game board, it's almost time to take your first look at the game in action. But before you do that, you need to add the game controller so there is something more to look at besides just a static screen.

Scroll through the list of actors and find the one named "game controller." Drag this Actor onto the Stage anywhere and drop it. You'll see it's the default Gamesalad actor, just a big, white square. This is fine for use as a game controller since the player will never see it. If you have deselected the game controller, **Single Click** it to activate it. **Drag** one of its corner resize points and make it much smaller, so small that you can move it off the Stage and place it on the pasteboard like in Figure 5.5.

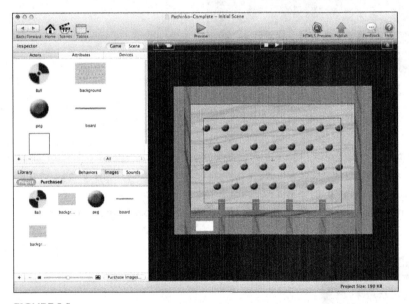

FIGURE 5.5
The Game Control actor placed on the pasteboard of the game board.

Typically, a game control actor is not placed in the live area of the stage so their appearance is meaningless. As long as the actor is placed somewhere on the stage, it's behaviors will run while the game is playing. The purpose of the game controller in the Pachinko game is only to spawn the players' ball as needed. **Click** the **Preview** button at the top of the Gamesalad window and check out how the game looks so far. Hopefully you see the completed game board with a blue ball hovering across the top of the screen (see Figure 5.1 above). **Click** the **Mouse** button anywhere in the stage area, the ball will drop and bounce off the pegs you took such great effort in placing. Eventually, the ball will come to rest on the board at the bottom of the screen.

Everything should be working just like it was planned in the rules of the game. But nothing brings a video game to life like sound; it sure would be nice to give the player a little audio feedback to liven the experience of playing the game. For the final step of building the game, you're going to add a new behavior that will play a bounce sound when the ball hits any solid surface. So far, we have only mentioned behaviors a couple times. In later chapters, you will spend a lot of time working with them since they are a cornerstone of Gamesalad.

Since it's the ball that is going to make the sound, you'll add the sound behavior to the ball actor. **Double-Click** the ball Actor to open its Actor Editor and then select the Sounds tab in the Library Palette. Your screen should look like Figure 5.6.

FIGURE 5.6
The Actor Editor for the Ball actor.

The right side of the screen contains all of the behaviors that the ball uses during the game. Don't worry if you don't know what these do yet; by the end of this book, you'll be able to customize them all and add your own to make the ball behave anyway you can imagine.

To add the new Behavior, **Click** the **Create Rule** button that is in the top right corner of the widow. This will add an empty Rule to the window (see Figure 5.7). It is a good idea to name Rules and Behaviors so **Double Click** the current name "Rule" and name it something more appropriate, like "Play Bounce Sound."

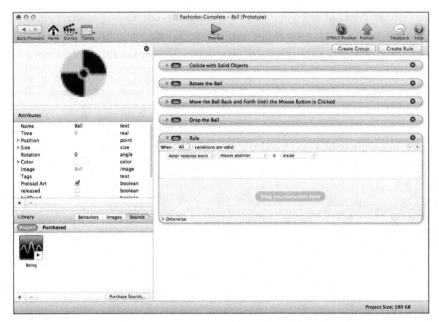

FIGURE 5.7
An empty Rule has been added to the ball actors list of Behaviors.

Next, change the drop-down menu that says "mouse position" to "overlaps or collides." When you do that, the menu structure will slightly change. In the new "Actor of type" menu that appears, select the option "Actor with tag." The last menu should auto-fill with "solid."

Now, **Click** the **Plus (+)** button in the upper right corner of this rule. Do not click the "X" button, that will delete the entire rule. The plus button will add a second series of conditions to the rule. First, change the drop-down menu that says "Actor receives event" to "Attribute." When you do this, a new empty box will appear. **Click** the **three dots** next to the empty box. A new window called "Attribute Browser" will open. **Click** the word **"Ball"** in the first column. In the second column that displays, scroll down to find the option "released." **Double-Click** this option and the window will close. Finally, drag the sound named "Boing" from the Sounds tab and drop it in the rule you just created where it says "Drag your Behaviors here." The completed behavior should look like Figure 5.8.

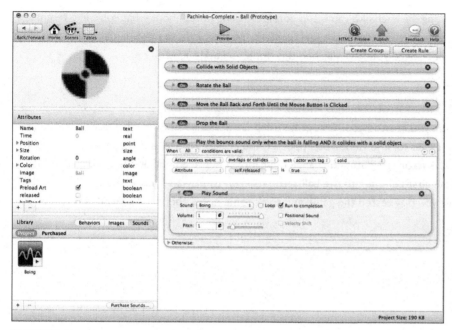

FIGURE 5.8
The completed "Play Bounce Sound" Rule.

Now, when you **Preview** the game, everything should be exactly like it was before, but this time there should be some sound!

Play Testing the Game

It is important to play your games as you develop them so you can continually make small edits and adjustments instead of leaving all the testing until the end of a project. As you worked through the steps of this chapter, you already had some experience play testing your game. Leaving all the editing towards the end can make things very difficult. You don't want to have too many things to fix at one time or else you may lose track of what you want to edit. Or worse yet, you may have introduced a bug early in the development process that is nearly impossible to track down at such a late date.

In addition to looking for errors (bugs) during testing, it is also important to consider what is fun about the game, what might not be fun, and what else could be added or changed to make the game even better. You want to make the best game you can. No matter how hard you worked on something, don't be afraid to change something in the game (or even throw something away) if it doesn't feel like it belongs in the game. It's a good idea to have other people play test your games as well—they will often find things you have missed or offer ideas you may not have considered.

Spend some time play testing the Pachinko game and consider taking notes about what you'd like to change or add to the project. Even though you may not feel comfortable adding these new elements now, you'll be able to return to the project, once you have finished this book, and add them.

Summary

While reading this chapter, you created your first game using Gamesalad. You used what you've learned so far to design and plan the rules for the game. You imported the images for use in the game and created the game board. You edited the actor attributes to change their look and placement on the gameboard. Then you added and edited your first behavior to the ball actor, telling it to play a sound when it collides with other solid actors. Finally, you play tested the game and took some notes about what you'd like to change.

Chapter 6
Attributes

In This Chapter, You Will Learn:

» How to use game, scene, and actor attributes

» The six different attributes types Gamesalad offers

» How to create custom attributes

» How to use operators to manipulate attributes

In this chapter, you will learn all about attributes, first by exploring the three "levels" Gamesalad uses to organize attributes. Then you will learn about the six attribute types you have to choose from and what each is used for. Finally, you'll learn about the three different types of operations that can be performed on attributes in games.

What Are Attributes?

Attributes are one of the most important concepts of Gamesalad. Even though you have spent a little time using them in the last couple of chapters, let's take a closer look at attributes and how they interact with each other.

Gamesalad offers three different "levels" of attributes: game level, scene level, and actor level attributes.

» **Game Attributes:** These are available for use in all scenes and by all actors in a game. Game level attributes can be thought of as the "top level" attributes. This top level is available for use by all the levels under it.

» **Scene Attributes:** These are scene-specific. The individual scene can access any of its own attributes and any actors within that same scene are able to access the scene attributes by unlocking an actor in that scene and making it an instance actor. The scene can access any of the game level attributes at any time.

» **Actor Attributes:** These are actor-specific. An actor can access its own attributes as needed. Actors are not able to directly access the attributes of other actors. To access scene level attributes, an actor MUST be an unlocked instance actor. Actors can access Game Level Attributes at any time.

Gamesalad separates attributes into these three categories to help cut down on clutter when you are developing a game and to help the game run more efficiently. When creating an attribute, carefully consider which "level" the attribute should be used in. If it is an attribute that will need to be accessed throughout the game, in many scenes by many actors, then it should be a game level attribute. An example would be an attribute that is used to keep track of a game's score—this would likely be displayed on-screen in many scenes as part of graphical user interface (GUI) and many actors may add to the score as they are destroyed or collected. On the other hand, an attribute that is only used by one actor, like an attribute that is used to set the speed of the actor, should be created as an actor level attribute only in the actor that needs it.

Game level attributes are kept in the computer's memory the entire time the game is being played; however, scene level and actor level attributes are "thrown away" once they are not needed anymore. By separating attributes into the correct levels, you will help the game run more smoothly and efficiently.

Attributes can be used to record numeric, text, or angle values. But it's what you do with these values that really make your games interesting and fun to play. When you create a new attribute, you should name it something meaningful. As your games get more complex, you don't want to have to sort through a list of attributes named "New Attribute 1," "New Attribute 2," "New Attribute 3," etc. As you complete the projects in this book, you'll learn a lot of uses for attributes and see just how important they are to a game's creation.

Attribute Types

There are six different types of attributes that can be used in Gamesalad.

» **Boolean:** This attribute stores a true or false value. When you create a new boolean attribute, you will be presented with a check box in the attribute list. A checked box will set the attribute to true while an unchecked box sets it to false. The boolean value's true and false are case sensitive and must be entered in any input boxes as lowercase.

» **Text:** This attribute type is used to record letters or numbers as characters. The default value for a text attribute is " ", an empty text box.

» **Integer:** Integers store positive or negative whole numbers (e.g. 100, -5, 9562). The default value of an integer attribute is 0.0. While this default value shows a decimal place, if you enter a decimal number, Gamesalad will round it up or down as needed.

» **Real:** This attribute type stores positive or negative decimal values (e.g. 0.023, -9.5, 3.0). The default value of an integer attribute is 0.0.

» **Angle:** Angles are used to keep track of angles of rotation and any positive value between 0 and 359 can be used, even decimal values (e.g. 6, 240, 90.5). The default value of an integer attribute is 0.0. If you enter a negative value, Gamesalad will automatically calculate the positive rotation of the number you entered.

» **Index:** The index attribute is used to store only positive whole numbers (e.g. 100, 5, 9562). The default value of an index attribute is 0.0. While this default value shows a decimal place, if you enter a decimal number, Gamesalad will round it up or down as needed. If you enter a negative number, Gamesalad keeps the value of 0.0.

Note: Booleans as Numbers

When entered in input boxes, boolean values can be input as the number 0 for false and 1 for true.

Where to Find Attributes

Game attributes are accessed through the inspector palette in the stage/scene editor. Let's take a look at the three "levels" of attributes. In the inspector palette, make sure the Game button and Attributes tab are active (see Figure 6.1).

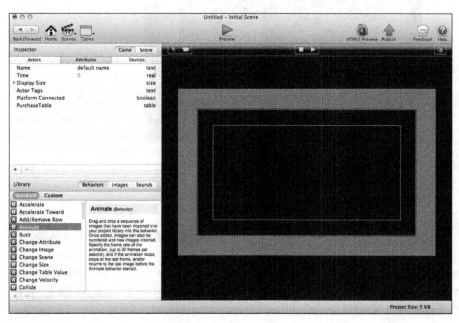

FIGURE 6.1
The Game Level Attributes Tab in the Inspector Palette.

Every game starts with the default game attributes, Name, Time, Display Size (Width and Height), Actor Tags, Platform Connected, and Purchase Table. At the bottom of this window is a plus (+) and minus (-) button—these are used to add or delete your own custom game attributes. Clicking the plus (+) button will display a list of available attribute types. Choose the type you want to create and press the choose button to add it the list. To delete an attribute, highlight it by single clicking it and pressing the minus (-) button. If the attribute is currently in use in the game, you will be presented with a message asking if you are sure you want to delete the attribute. You are not able to delete any of the default game, scene, or actor attributes.

To access the scene attributes, **Click** the **Scene** button and you will see the following window (Figure 6.2).

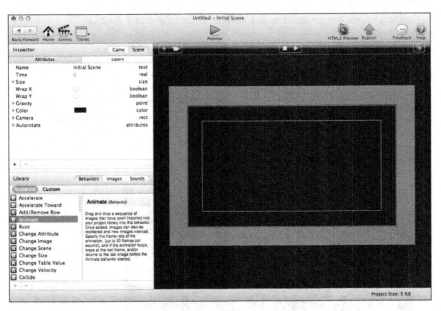

FIGURE 6.2
The Scene Level Attributes Tab in the Inspector Palette.

You can add and delete your own custom attributes from this list with the plus (+) and minus (-) buttons.

To see a list of the actor Attributes, you'll need to add an actor to the game by returning to the Actors tab of the Game Inspector. Use the **Plus (+)** button to add an actor and **Double-Click** this actor to enter its editor (see Figure 6.3). You've already spent some time with the actor attributes, so you should be familiar with this list.

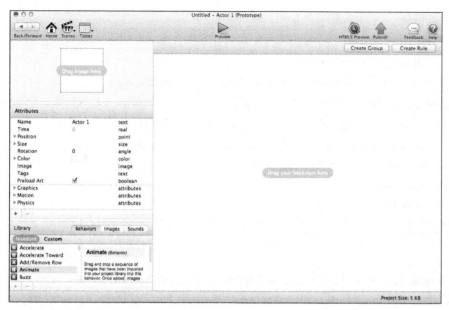

FIGURE 6.3
The Actor Level Attributes in the actor editor.

NOTE: Attribute Meanings

It is beyond the scope of this book to outline and describe each and every default attribute at the game, scene, and actor levels. As you work through this book, you'll gain an understanding of many of them and what is not covered is outlined on the Gamesalad website (https://help.gamesalad.com/hc/en-us/articles/202699556-1-11-Glossary).

Operators

Once you have a list of attributes created, to use them to their fullest potential, you'll need to perform some calculations or comparisons on them to modify them. In Gamesalad, you can perform arithmetic operations, text operations, and equality operations on attributes. Operators are applied using Gamesalad's behaviors. Later in this book, you'll look at many of the behaviors Gamesalad has and learn how to use them in conjunction with attributes.

Arithmetic Operations

Standard math operations are performed on attributes using arithmetic operators. Table 6.1 describes Gamesalad's arithmetic operators.

Table 6.1 Arithmetic Operators

Operator	Description
+	Addition. Adds two numbers together.
-	Subtraction. Reduces the number on the left by the number on the right.
*	Multiplication. Multiplies two numbers together.
/	Division. Divides the number on the left by the number on the right.
%	Modulus. Divides the number on the left by the number on the right, but returns the remainder instead of the result. For example: 20 % 5 will return 0 17 % 3 will return 2 8 % 5 will return 3

Text Operations

While text attributes are typically used to store words or letters, if you do use them to store numbers, you are able to use all of the arithmetic operators listed above on numeric text attributes. If you try to perform arithmetic operations on a mix of numeric and letter text attributes, you will get an error. Table 6.2 describes Gamesalad's text operator.

Table 6.2 Text Operators

Operator	Description
..	Concatenation. This operator will combine two text attributes. For example: "Hello".."World" will return HelloWorld

Equality Operators

Equality operators compare two numeric or text values and return a true or false value. Equality operators are used in rules and loops, both of which you'll learn about in the behaviors sections later in this book. Table 6.3 describes the equality operators.

Table 6.3 Equality Operators for Numeric Values

Operator	Description
=	Equal to. Returns a true value if the two values are equal and false if they are not. For example: 2 = 2 will return true 8 = 14 will return false

Operator	Description
≠	Not equal to. Returns a true value if the two values are not the same and false if they are. For example: 6 ≠ 7 will return true 4 ≠ 4 will return false
<	Less than. Returns a true value if the value on the left is less than the value on the right and false if it is not. 9 < 3 will return false 3 < 60 will return true
>	Greater than. Returns a true value if the value on the left is more than the value on the right and true if it is not. 9 > 3 will return true 3 > 60 will return false
≤	Less than or equal to. Will return a value of true if the value on the left is less than or equal to the value on the right and false if it is not. 9 ≤ 9 will return true 30 ≤ 8 will return false
≥	Greater than or equal to. Will return a value of true if the value on the left is more than or equal to the value on the right and false if it is not. 9 ≥ 9 will return true 30 ≥ 8 will return true

Table 6.4 Equality Operators for Text Values (these are case sensitive)

Operator	Description
Contains	If the text attribute on the left contains the text on the right, the value returned will be true, otherwise it will be false. "Hello World" contains "rld" will return true "Happy Birthday" contains "15th" will return false
Begins with	If the text attribute on the left begins with the text on the right, a value of true will be returned, otherwise it will be false. "Gamesalad is Fun" begins with "Game" will return true "Gamesalad is Fun" begins with "game" will return false

Operator	Description
Ends with	If the text attribute on the left ends with the text on the right, the value returned will be true, otherwise it will be false. "This book is great" ends with "Great" will return false "What?" ends with "?" will return true
Is	If the text attribute on the left matches the text on the right, the value returned will be true, otherwise it will be false. "Hello World" is "Hello World" returns true "Hello World" is "hello" returns false

Summary

In this chapter, you learned about the three "levels" of attributes in Gamesalad and how to determine which "level" custom attributes should be created at. You then learned about the six different types of attributes and when to use each type. Finally, you finished the hour by learning about the three types of operations Gamesalad can perform on attributes. You also reviewed some examples of each operation.

Chapter 7
Graphics and Artwork

In This Chapter You Will Learn:

» What file types Gamesalad supports for images

» How to create artwork at the correct size

» What resolution independence is

» What color spaces are

» How to create images with a transparent background

This chapter is all about images and how to get the most out of them. First, you'll learn what file format Gamesalad uses for images. Then you will learn what pixel dimensions are and how they influence the look of your images and the performance of your games. Next, you will learn about resolution independence and why this is important when creating games for Apple iOS devices. You will also learn about image color space and transparency. Finally, you'll learn a few ways to get images for your projects if you are not an artist.

Graphics

Nothing brings more life to a video game than the graphics and images used to create the sprites, backgrounds, and special effects in the game. The graphics can set the mood of the game from a lighthearted cartoon to a dark and frightening nightmare. The style of the graphics used in your games is, of course, entirely up to you as the designer, but there are some graphical specifications that you should be aware of while you are creating or commissioning the artwork.

File Type

Gamesalad supports the PNG file format for images. Images can be created as any file format in an image editor, but Gamesalad will convert them to PNG files while importing them. During the conversion process, it is possible that colors may shift or other unexpected results might occur. For this reason, you should always export your own PNG files from the image editor. When you export the PNG files, you will have complete control over things like compression, color space, image quality, etc.

NOTE: Image Editors

While the image editor pictured in this section is Adobe Photoshop, there are many other image editors available that can perform the same functions. Many indie developers use GIMP since it is very capable and, best of all, it's free!

Only the file you are going to import into Gamesalad needs to be a PNG file. While you are creating images, you can work in any file format you prefer. A typical workflow for creating an image for use in Gamesalad is outlined below:

1. Sketch the image on paper or on a tablet.
2. Import that sketch into Adobe Illustrator and use it as a guide to create the image.
3. Open the Adobe Illustrator vector file in Adobe Photoshop and add any special effects or tweaks that can't be created in Illustrator.
4. Export the final file as a PNG file for use in Gamesalad.

Note: Vector Files

I like to start all of my artwork in Adobe Illustrator. Since it is a vector art program, the artwork can be resized as needed, large or small, without losing any image quality. The vector files can even be used for print, marketing and video graphics.

Pixel Dimensions

Individual graphics and frames of animation should be created in even-numbered pixel ratios that are divisible by 4. If graphic elements are kept within these dimensions, they will always look good on-screen and be optimized for use in Gamesalad:

8 x 8 pixels
16 x 16 pixels
32 x 32 pixels
64 x 64 pixels
128 x 128 pixels
256 x 256 pixels
512 x 512 pixels
1024 x 1024 pixels
2048 x 2048 pixels

Note: Pixels

A pixel, or picture element, is the smallest unit of color information that makes up an image on a digital screen and is typically a square. The number of pixels in an image is known as the image's resolution.

Following the above ratios, you can also safely create images that are rectangles, as well as squares, by combining different heights and widths of pixels like 32 x 64 pixels, 8 x 256 pixels, 1024 x 512 pixels, etc. (see Figure 7.1A-B).

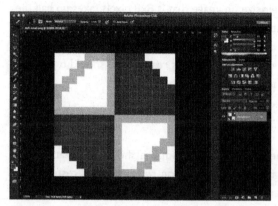

FIGURE 7.1A
A square (16x16 pixel) image in Photoshop.

FIGURE 7.1B
A rectangular (128x64 pixel) image in Photoshop.

There are two reasons you should keep images sized to these dimensions. The images will be optimized for viewing on-screen and not pixelate or look blurry. They will also be optimized for the device's memory usage. When viewed on a screen, images that meet these requirements will look sharp and crisp. However, if you were to create an image that is 16 x 17 pixels (instead of 16 x 16), the image may be blurry and pixelated when displayed in a game.

Each image used in a game uses up a portion of the device's memory it is displayed on. As games increase in size and complexity, it is very possible that they may slow the device down and cause the game to run slow or even crash. As the developer, it is your responsibility to manage your use of memory as much as possible. Images take up a "block" of memory equal to their size; an image that is 8x8 pixels takes up half the memory of an image that is 16x16 pixels. But if you create an image that is 16x17 pixels, it will take up as much memory as an image that is 16x32 pixels because of the single extra pixel. Since the image has an extra pixel, it is forced to fill up the next largest "block" of memory. For this reason, you should try to minimize the pixel dimensions of your images without sacrificing image or game quality.

Resolution Independence

If you plan on publishing games for Apple devices (iPhone, iPad, Macintosh), images should be created so they can be viewed at their best quality on retina (high resolution) and non-retina (normal resolution) screens. Since a retina screen has a much higher pixel density than standard screens, images appear much smoother and the individual pixels can't be seen at a normal viewing distance.

When creating images for display on Apple devices, you should create the pixel image, the PNG file, at twice the pixel size you'll want the actor to display in the game. For example, if you want a ball actor in a game to be 32x32 pixels, you'll need to create the PNG file for this actor at a size of 64x64 pixels.

Exercise 4

Creating and Importing a Resolution Independent Image

In this exercise, you will create a resolution independent image for use on an Apple device. You'll first create the image in an image editor and then import it and apply it to an actor in Gamesalad.

Let's create the ball image I mention above. The actor will be 32x32 pixels in Gamesalad so you'll want the image file to be 64x64 pixels.

1. Open your favorite image editor; I'll be using Adobe Photoshop for this exercise.
2. Start a new image project and set the Width and Height to 64 pixels and the Resolution to 72 pixels per inch. If you're able, choose RGB for the color mode and Transparent for the background (see Figure 7.2).

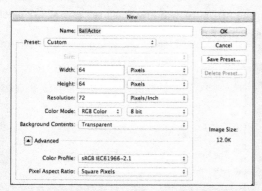

FIGURE 7.2
Adobe Photoshops project creation dialog box.

3. Create a ball image in the window provided. The ball does not need to be fancy, just create something to test it with.

4. Export the image as a PNG file. If you are using Photoshop, go to the **File** Menu and choose **Save for Web**. In the dialog box that appears (see Figure 7.3), chose **PNG-24** as the file type and make sure the pixel dimensions are 64x64.

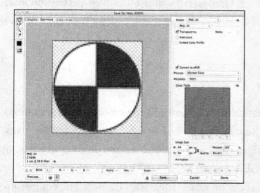

FIGURE 7.3
Adobe Photoshops "Save for Web" dialog box.

5. Next, open Gamesalad and start a new project. Make sure to choose one of the iPad or iPhone project types and check Resolution Independence.

6. Navigate to the Stage and activate the Images tab in the Library palette.

7. **Click** the **Plus (+)** button and import the ball image you just created.

8. To create the Actor, drag this image into the Actor tab of the Inspector palette above and release it.

9. **Double-Click** the Actor and check its size in the Attribute Window. You'll see it is 32x32 pixels, half the pixel dimensions of the image file (see Figure 7.4).

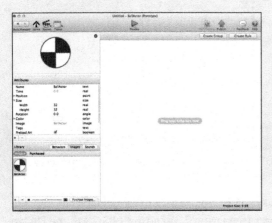

FIGURE 7.4
The resolution independent image applied to an actor in Gamesalad.

When you publish a game using resolution independence, Gamesalad will use the high-resolution image to create a low-resolution image for use on non-retina devices so the game will look its best on whatever device it is played on.

Color Space

Color space, also known as color model, is a mathematical description of how colors are represented. There are many different color models; RGB, CMYK, hexadecimal, all of which have their specific uses, like printing and displaying colors on web pages. While images can be created using any color space that the image editor supports, it is best to create art as an RGB file from the start. That way, when the final image is exported as a PNG file, there will not be any color shifts or other surprises. Gamesalad requires images to be in the RGB color space. If the image being imported is saved using a color space other than RGB, Gamesalad will convert the image to RGB during the import process.

NOTE: Color Shift

A color shift can occur when an image is transformed between different color spaces. Each color space uses a different calculation, or mix of numbers, to represent colors. It is possible that one color space will represent a given color differently than another color space. For example, bright blues in the RGB color space typically appear very dull when viewed in the CMYK color space.

Transparency

Every image created in an image editor is going to be a rectangle. There are a specific number of pixels for the image's height and width (32x32, 256x8, etc.)—this is called the image's "canvas." While every canvas must be a rectangle, you can use image transparency to make images appear to be other shapes in Gamesalad. The ball image you've used several times so far uses image transparency to make the ball look like a circle, even though the image imported into Gamesalad is actually a square.

Exercise 5

Image Transparency

In this exercise, you'll learn how image transparency works.

1. Open the image named "LargeBall.png" in an image editor. The file can be found in the book asset files for Chapter 7 folder.

2. The image size is a square, 256x256 pixels, but the ball image is a circle. In Photoshop, you can check an image's size by choosing **Image Size...** from the **Image** menu.

3. The gray and white checkerboard at the four corners of the ball indicates that area is transparent; this is common in most image editors (see Figure 7.5).

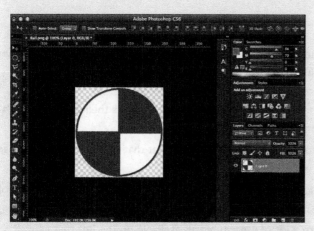

FIGURE 7.5
Adobe Photoshops transparent background
'checker board pattern'.

4. When exporting a PNG image with transparency, it must be saved as a 32-bit file. In Photoshop, choosing PNG-24 as the file format will do this (see Figure 7.6).

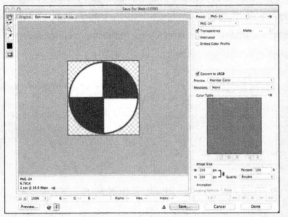

FIGURE 7.6
Exporting an image with a transparent background from Adobe Photoshop as a PNG-24 file.

5. When this image with transparency is imported into Gamesalad, it will look like a circle even though the actual image is a square.

Not an Artist?

If you're not an artist, and you don't have any members of your team who are, you're probably wondering how to get image files for your games. Don't worry; there are lots of options:

» **Gamesalad Marketplace:** As mentioned earlier in the book, Gamesalad has their own marketplace that you are able to purchase images from.

» **Stock Image Sites:** There are many stock image sites on the Internet that have art and other assets available for sale, or even for free.

» **Hire an Artist:** Many great artists work for hire and will be happy to work with you on your game projects.

» **Become an Artist:** Creating simple 2D artwork does not have to be difficult. If you are interested in learning to create your own art, there are a lot of great tutorials available on the Internet as well.

Note: How NOT to Source Images

DO NOT do a Google search for images and just pull them off of the Internet. Most of the artwork you will find by doing a Google search is copyrighted by its creator. It is illegal and un-ethical to use such art in games (or any project) without first asking the author for permission.

Summary

In this chapter, you learned all about images. You learned what file type, color space, and pixel dimension to use when creating images. You also learned about resolution independence and how Gamesalad uses one image to create a high and low-resolution version for use on Apple devices. Then you learned about how to create an image with a transparent background so not all of your images have to look like rectangles. Finally, you learned about various ways to get artwork for your games if you are not artistically inclined.

Chapter 8
Behaviors Part 1

In This Chapter You Will Learn:

» What behaviors are

» The three types of behaviors available

» How to add behaviors to an actor

» How to organize behaviors

Thus far, you have learned how to create a project in Gamesalad, how to add scenes to a project, and how to add actors to those scenes. In this chapter, you will begin to learn what behaviors are and how to use them to bring actors to life. Through Gamesalad's behavior system, you can add complex interactions to your actors to build just about any kind of game you can imagine. You'll begin by learning behavior basics— you'll learn how to add them to actors and start experimenting and play testing some of the most commonly used behaviors.

Behaviors

Behaviors are Gamesalad's system of coding or scripting. While you won't do any traditional programming in Gamesalad, a lot of the concepts associated with behaviors are very similar to those of programming. Luckily, Gamesalad has done all of the heavy lifting for you—the behavior system is entirely based on a drag and drop concept. You'll drag pre-established bits of "code" into your actors and often fill in a few choices, check boxes, or pull down menus and your behaviors will be ready to run.

Behaviors can be used to control an actor's movement, change an actor's appearance, control interactions between actors, and do just about anything else you can imagine. Don't let Gamesalad fool you. While its drag and drop system is easy to pick up and work with as a new user, it has enough power and flexibility to create a professional-quality game that can hold its own in any app store.

Note: Successful Gamesalad Games
Gamesalad has been used to create more than 80 of the top 100 games published in the U.S. Apple App Store and three #1 games have been created with Gamesalad!

As of this writing, Gamesalad ships with 53 standard behaviors. If you are a Pro-user, there are four additional pro behaviors included with your license. This chapter, and the two that follow it, will examine the most commonly used standard behaviors.

Behavior Types

Gamesalad offers 3 different types of behaviors:

» **Persistent Behaviors:** These are Behaviors that will continuously act on an actor during gameplay. The letter "B" preceding the behavior's name on the list indicates a persistent behavior (see Figure 8.1).

FIGURE 8.1
The Standard Behaivor list in the Library Palette.

» **Action Behaviors:** Action behaviors occur only one time when activated by an actor. The letter "A" preceding the behavior's name on the list indicates an action behavior.
» **Container Behaviors:** Container behaviors literally hold other behaviors. With these containers, you can build a complex series of behaviors that are only executed at a specific time or when certain conditions are met. The letter "G" preceding the behavior's name on the list indicates a container behavior.

Behaviors Tab

The behaviors tab in the library palette lists standard and custom behaviors. If you are a pro-user, you will also see an option for pro behaviors. The standard list contains all of the behaviors you have access to as a free user and the custom list is for storing your own container behaviors. When you highlight (by single clicking) any behavior on the list, the right side of the palette will fill with a definition of the behavior and some specific information about its use.

Note: Definitions

In this chapter, and the next two, you'll be learning about many of the behaviors on the list. For those behaviors that aren't covered, you should take time to read the information that Gamesalad provides in the definitions box.

Creating Behavior Lists

Let's get to learning about behaviors and how to build your own game using them. To begin, open the file named "Behaviors Demo" provided with the book files for chapter 8. This file is a simple project with one actor already created; you'll use this actor to learn about behaviors first-hand. Once you have the file open, **Double-Click** the actor and add a few behaviors to get things going.

1.   **Drag** an Accelerate Behavior into the window that displays "Drag your Behaviors here." This area of the editor is known as the behavior editor (this area will contain all of the actors behaviors and rules).

Note: Behavior Order

The list of behaviors in the library palette is alphabetically organized. The accelerate behavior is first on the list.

---

2.   Don't make any changes to the default settings of the accelerate behavior, just press the **Preview button** at the top of the window and see what you have just created.

3.   As you can see, an accelerate behavior moves the actor in a given direction at a certain acceleration. To change the direction and speed the actor is moving, press the **Back button** to return to the Actors editor. Update the settings in the Accelerate Behavior so the number 90 is in the Direction field. Reduce the Acceleration to 10. Press **Preview** again, you'll now see the actor is moving at a much slower rate, up the screen instead of to the left.

In addition to typing a value into the direction field of the accelerate behavior, you are also able to rotate the small circle located within the large circle next to the direction field to set the value (see Figure 8.2). Click and drag the small circle around and see how the direction field updates.

FIGURE 8.2
The Accelerate Behavior.

Note: Directions

Gamesalad uses degrees of rotation to represent direction with the default direction always being 0 (right). Rotating counter-clockwise around a circle, 90 is up, 180 is left, and 270 is down.

Stacking Behaviors

You are able to "stack" behaviors in an actors behavior editor. As you add behaviors to the list, each behavior will be acted on according to the settings you apply. Gamesalad begins at the top of the behaviors list and executes each behaviors in order from top to bottom. Through the use of "special" behaviors (timers, rules, and loops), it's possible to interrupt this top-to-bottom execution of behaviors. Let's stack some behaviors:

1. Using the actor you created in the previous steps, make sure the Accelerate Behavior is set up with a Direction of 90 and an Acceleration of 10. This time, select the Scene option from the "Relative to:" menu.
2. Next, add a Rotate Behavior below the Accelerate Behavior in the list. Remember, the behaviors list is alphabetical.
3. Press **Preview** and you'll see the actor is now rotating counter-clockwise AND moving at the same time.

Note: Relative To

Several behaviors have the option of applying their settings relative to the actor or the scene (see Figure 8.2 above). Remember the scene and each actor have their own unique sets of coordinates—the "relative to" choice is effectively telling Gamesalad which coordinate system to use for the behavior. The choice "relative to: actor" will apply the action relative to the actors coordinate system and the "relative to: scene" will apply the action relative to the scenes coordinate system.

---

4. Return to the Actors editor by pressing the Back button. Drag a Change Size Attribute to the bottom of the list and set the Growth Rate to 0.1.
5. When you **Preview**, you'll see that the actor now slowly grows in size as it moves and rotates.

Behavior Controls

As the list of behaviors grows, organization will become paramount. While the list you have built at the moment only contains three behaviors (Accelerate, Rotate, and Change Size), when you build more complex actions, the actors will likely contain many more behaviors. There are several controls you can use on each behavior to keep the list readable (see Figure 8.3).

» **Expand/Collapse:** Click the arrow to the left of the behavior name to expand or collapse its settings.

» **On/Off:** Clicking this button will toggle the behaviors settings on and off. A behavior that is turned off will have no effect during gameplay.

» **Delete (x) Button:** Clicking this button will delete the behavior from the list. When a behavior is deleted, it will no longer perform its action. You can also delete a behavior by activating the behavior (clicking it once) and pressing the Delete key on the keyboard.

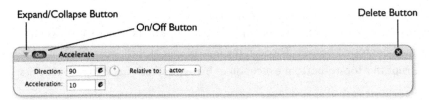

FIGURE 8.3
The behavior controls.

The order of behaviors can be changed at any time by dragging and dropping them to a new location in the list.

Behavior Naming

While each behavior is automatically named for its action, this can be very vague and not very helpful once you have a long list of behaviors that build very complex actions. It's a good idea to give each of the behaviors a descriptive name so you are able to read through the list and know exactly what's going on, even if the behaviors details are collapsed. This is known as commenting your code and is worth taking the time to do.

Exercise 6

Behavior Organization

Practice some of the organization techniques mentioned above.

1. Using the list of behaviors you just built, **Double-Click** and edit each name as shown in Figure 8.4.

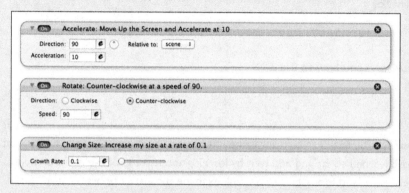

FIGURE 8.4
The list of behaviors with more descriptive names.

2. Next, **Click** and **Drag** the Change Size Behavior to the top of the list.
3. Then, use the Expand/Collapse arrow to collapse all of the Behavior details.
4. Finally, press the On/Off button on the Rotate Behavior so it becomes inactive.
5. Even though the behaviors are now closed, you should still be able to read the names and understand what each one does.
6. **Preview** the action and note that the actor no longer rotates as it moves since you have turned that behavior off.

Summary

In this chapter, you learned what behaviors are and how to add them to actors. You experimented with a few of the behavior types and play tested a project, getting first- hand experience with behaviors. Then you learned how to adjust behavior settings. Finally, you learned how to organize behaviors so you are able to understand the flow of the project and what each actors action will be just by reading the list.

Chapter 9
Behaviors Part 2

In This Chapter You Will Learn:

» How to use a timer behavior

» How to create rules

» How to create loops

» What the attribute browser is and how to use it

In the last chapter, you learned the basics of creating game interactions by using behaviors. In this chapter, you will take what you have learned so far and add to it by learning about some of the more complex container behaviors, timers, rules, and loops. Finally, you will examine the attribute browser and learn how actors can access all of the attributes used in a game.

Tip: Sample File

Just like in the previous chapter, there is a sample file for use with this chapter's lessons. The file is named "Behaviors Demo 2" and is located in the Assets Folder for Chapter 9.

Container Behaviors

A container behavior is literally a behavior that must contain other behaviors in order to perform a function. Container behaviors are used to trigger events only when certain conditions are met. Each type of container behavior has a specific set of conditions it is able to use.

» **Timer:** A timer will perform any behaviors it has access to at specifically timed intervals. Timers can perform their behaviors "every x number of seconds," "after x number of seconds," or "for x number of seconds," where x is a real number.

» **Rule:** A rule will execute behaviors when a certain set of user-established conditions are met. These conditions can be actions taken by the player or when an attribute changes within the game. In addition to executing behaviors when the conditions are met, rules can also trigger behaviors when certain conditions are not met. Rules are very similar to if/then/else statements used in traditional computer programming.

» **Loop:** A loop is very similar to a rule in that it will execute behaviors when a certain set of user-established conditions are met. However, a loop will repeatedly execute those behaviors, whereas a rule will execute behaviors only once.

» **Loop Over Table:** This container will repeatedly execute behaviors to a table. Tables are very similar to a spreadsheet; you will examine tables and some of their uses later in this book.

» **Group:** The group behavior itself doesn't perform any actions; groups are used to help organize your behaviors into logical order.

Timer Behavior

Timer behaviors will execute any behaviors included in them at set intervals of time. There are three options for timing: *every*, *after*, and *for* a given number of seconds. To learn about the timer behavior first hand, Open the file named "Behaivors Demo" that is provided in the game assets folder for Chapter 9 and **Double-Click** the actor named "Ball" in the Initial Scene (these actors should look familiar).

1. With the Ball Actor Editor open, scroll through the list of Behaviors in the Library Palette and Drag a Timer Behavior into the Behavior Editor. You may have noticed the scene was already built for you, with the ball actor placed at the top and a board actor placed at the bottom of the stage. You're going set this timer to drop the ball after one second so it falls down the screen towards the board at the bottom.

2. In the Timer Behavior, choose After from the Drop-Down Menu and enter a 1 in the Input Box.

3. If you were to Preview this now, nothing would happen because you haven't actually instructed Gamesalad to do anything yet. To complete the Timer Behavior, **Drag** an Accelerate Behavior into the Timer Behavior where it says "Drag your behaviors here."

4. In the Accelerate Behavior, change the Direction to 270 and choose Scene from the Relative to menu (see Figure 9.1).

Note: Nesting

Behaviors that are placed inside a container behavior are often referred to as being nested inside the behavior.

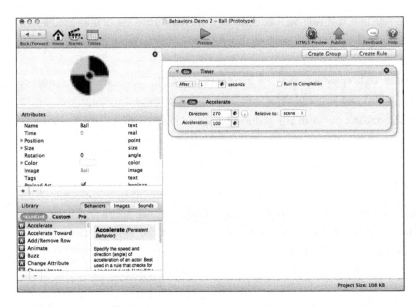

FIGURE 9.1
The completed timer behavior with a nested accelerate behavior.

Preview the scene and note how the ball starts to move only after one second passes. Wouldn't it be great if the ball hit the floorboard at the bottom of the scene and bounced? It only takes one behavior to make that happen.

Return to the Ball Actor's Editor and add a Collide behavior (do not nest this behavior in the timer) from the Behaviors list in the Library Palette. In this Collide Behavior, change the two drop-down menus to read "actor of type:" and "board," then replay the scene. Now, when the ball hits the board, it bounces!

Next, return to the Ball Actor Editor and delete the Accelerate Behavior from the Timer (don't delete the timer behavior itself). Nest a Move Behavior in the Timer where the Accelerate Behavior had been. Set the Move Behavior's Direction to 270, Speed to 100, and choose scene from the Relative to menu. Next, change the Timer Behavior so it reads "For 2.25 seconds." **Preview** the scene. This time, the ball will immediately begin to drop down the scene, but it will stop after 2.25 seconds, before it ever comes in contact with the floor board.

Tip: Behavior Play Time

One of the best ways to learn about all of the behaviors available in Gamesalad is to create a "play" file similar to this one and add behaviors to your actors. Try their different settings, in different combinations, and watch what happens.

As you can see, with a few simple behaviors and settings, you are able to easily create interactive elements using Gamesalad. While you only added one behavior to the timer behavior, you are able to stack behaviors inside all of the container behaviors to build complex interactions, just like you can in the main behavior editor.

Rules

Rules are very similar to the traditional programming concept of if/then/else statements. Rules use a series of conditions to determine what to do within a game. While the game can only make a single decision at one time, if you string several conditions together, you can build very complex and detailed interactions in a game. The rule behavior has a few more options than the timer behavior. Let's take a look at the contents of an empty rule (see Figure 9.2).

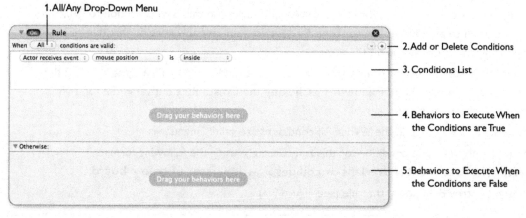

FIGURE 9.2
An empty rule.

1. Rules can be created to take effect when *All* or *Any* of the conditions established are met.
2. All rules must have at least one condition. To add or delete conditions, use the plus (+) and minus (-) buttons.
3. The conditions you establish will always return a true of false value to the rule.
    a. When a rule is created to take effect when *All* conditions are valid, all conditions listed must return true for the rule to perform its function.
    b. When a rule is created to take effect when *Any* of its conditions are valid, only one of the conditions listed must return true for the rule to perform its function.

4. Behaviors added to this area of the rule will take effect when the conditions you have established are met.

5. Behaviors added to the Otherwise area take effect when the conditions you have established are not met.

Exercise 7

Rules

In this exercise, you will playtest a rule to see how all of these concepts fit together. If you have closed it, Open the same file you were working with for the timers section of this chapter. Delete any current Behaviors in the Ball Actor.

1. First, add an Accelerate Behavior to the Ball Actor and set the values of Direction to 270, Acceleration to 50, and Relative to scene. By now, you can probably imagine that this behavior will simply move the ball down the screen.

2. Next, add a Rule to this list of Behaviors. You can either add a rule by **Dragging** it out of the Behaviors list in the Library Palette or by **Clicking** the Create Rule button in the top right corner of the actor editor.

3. Make sure All is chosen in the "When All conditions are valid:" menu.

4. You will only need one condition for this rule. Create it using the following format:
    Actor receives event » overlaps or collides » with » actor of type » board

5. Nest a Destroy Behavior in the rule (see Figure 9.3).

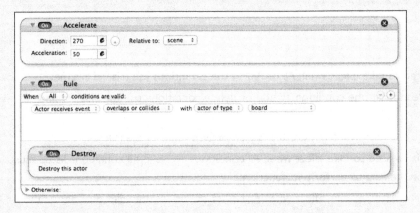

FIGURE 9.3
The completed behaviors.

Note: Behaviors Format

For the remainder of this book, when there is a series of menus or input boxes written out, it will be done in the
format above. Each menu or text choice will be separated by a "»" symbol.

Preview the scene and watch the action. Hopefully, the ball dropped down the screen and disappeared
when it touched the floorboard at the bottom. As you already know, the accelerate behavior moves the
ball down the screen while the rule handled the rest of the action. Conditions in rules usually can be
translated into a plain English statement. In this case, the condition states "When the ball actor touches
the board actor," execute the behaviors nested in the rule. The destroy behavior literally removes the ball
actor from the scene.

Conditions can be established to cover almost any situation imaginable. Throughout this book, you'll be
spending a lot of time learning much more about rules and their options.

Loops

Loops are very similar to rules. Loops will repeatedly execute the behaviors placed in them until their
given conditions are met, whereas rules only execute their behaviors once. The process of looping a series
of behaviors is also called "iteration." Gamesalad offers two different types of loops: *While* and *Until* loops.

» A While Loop will execute its behaviors while its conditions are true. Once the conditions become false,
the actions will cease.
» An Until Loop will execute its behaviors while its conditions are false. Once its conditions become true,
the actions will cease.

The structure of the loop behavior is very similar to that of a rule (see Figure 9.4).

1.   In order for the behaviors to execute, choose the loop type (*While* or *Until*) and decide if *All* or *Any*
of the conditions should be met.
2.   The plus (+) and minus (-) buttons will add or remove conditions.
3.   Establish the conditions needed for the loop.
4.   Nest the loops behaviors here.

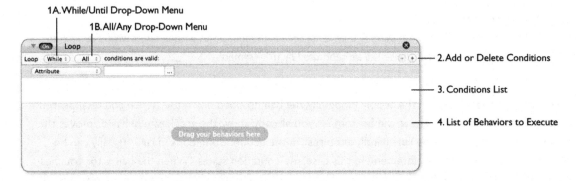

1A. While/Until Drop-Down Menu

1B. All/Any Drop-Down Menu

2. Add or Delete Conditions

3. Conditions List

4. List of Behaviors to Execute

FIGURE 9.4
An empty loop behavior.

Exercise 8

Loops

Using the same file from the rules exercise above, delete any behaviors in the ball to start with a blank slate. While building the loop below, you will be using the attribute browser and expression editor. In later chapters, these will both be examined in detail–just follow along for now and things will make more sense at the end of this chapter.

1. Add a Loop Behavior to the Ball.
2. Choose *While* and *All* for the loop type.
3. To set up the condition, **Click** the button to the right of the input field–it looks like 3 dots (…). This will open a dialog box known as the Attribute Browser.
a. **Click** Game in the first column.
b. **Double-Click** Time in the second column (this column will only appear after clicking Game).
c. Choose less than (<) from the drop-down menu that appears.
d. Enter the number 10 in the input box.
4. Next, nest a Change Attribute Behavior into the Behaviors section of the loop.
5. **Click** the (…) button next to the first input field and **Click** Ball in the first column.
a. **Click** Position in the second column and then **Double-Click** "X" in the third column when it appears.

6. **Click** the button on the right side of the next input field; it looks like a lowercase "e." This will open another dialog box known as the Expression Editor.

7. **Click** the Arrow Button in the lower left corner of the expression editor. From the list that appears, **Click** Ball, then **Click** Position, and then **Double-Click** "X".

8. Next to the blue oval that appears in the input box that reads "self.Position.X," type +1 (see Figure 9.5).

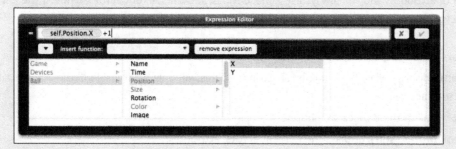

FIGURE 9.5
The Expression Editor.

9. Finally, **Click** the green check mark in the upper right corner of the Expression Editor.

10. The final Loop should look like Figure 9.6:

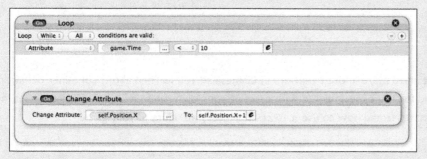

FIGURE 9.6
The completed Loop Behavior.

If put into plain English, this loop is saying "While the game has been running for less than ten seconds, move the ball actor one pixel to the right."

Preview the scene. The ball should now move to the right for the first ten seconds of the game. Once the condition of the loop becomes false (the game has been running for more than ten seconds), the ball stops.

Attribute Browser

While setting up the loop behavior, you spent some time in the attribute browser. The attribute browser gives your behaviors access to all of the attributes used throughout the game and is always reached by pressing the (...) button next to an input field.

The attribute browser is separated into four columns that auto fill as selections are made. The first column is the main level of attributes and will always list game, devices, and the current actor's name. If the current actor is an unlocked instance actor, this column will also display the current scene attributes.

» **Game:** displays all of the game level attributes.
» **Current Scene:** displays all of the scene level attributes (this will only be available IF the actor is an unlocked, instance actor).
» **Devices:** displays all of the devices' attributes.
» **Current actor name (self):** displays the current actors' attributes.

The attribute browser displays both the default attributes every Gamesalad game starts with and all of the custom attributes added while developing the game. By directly manipulating these attributes, you are able to control every aspect of a game from an actor's position on-screen (like we did in the loop above) to how many of those actors should appear on any given level of the game and for how long–the possibilities are truly endless.

Summary

In this chapter, you learned more about behaviors in Gamesalad. You learned about container behaviors and what each is used for. You experimented with creating your own rules and loops. Finally, you learned about the attribute browser and how to use it to control every attribute in your game.

Chapter 10
Player Input

In This Chapter You Will Learn:

» What player input is and how to add it to a game

» How to build keyboard controls for a game

» How to add mouse controls to a project

» How to add touch controls to mobile game projects

» How to accept text input

In order to actually play a game, a player has to have some way of giving input to the game. This input can take many forms; there are keyboards and mice, gamepads and joysticks, touch screens and motion controls on modern mobile devices, and many other forms of input. In this chapter, you will learn how to allow different forms of player input so people are able to actually play the great games you create.

Types of Input

Gamesalad projects are able to accept several different types of player input, these are:

» **Keyboard:** To determine if a specific key has been pressed, you'll use keyboard input. You'll have access to the full keyboard to set up the game controls.

» **Mouse:** In addition to using a keyboard to capture input from the player, you may want to use the mouse. With a mouse, you are able to capture the position of the mouse pointer on-screen and the state of the mouse button, up or down.

» **Touch:** Mobile devices are able to capture touch events as player input. Touches can be pressed, released, and inside or outside of an actor.

» **Accelerometer:** The accelerometer can also be used on mobile devices. The accelerometer determines the angle and rate of movement of the device and is useful for knowing when the player tilts or rotates their device.

» **Text:** Gamesalad is also able to accept input as actual text; this, of course, uses the keyboard. In this case, the player uses the keyboard to input text as a string of characters (e.g. entering their name in a high score list).

Keyboard Input

Keyboard input is generally set up using a rule, or a series of rules, for the various keys that can be used during a game. Keyboard input can be used for many things in a game; one of the most common is for player movement and control.

Exercise 9

Reading Keyboard Input

In this exercise, you will create keyboard controls to move an actor left and right on the stage:

1. Open the file named "Input" that is provided in the assets for Chapter 10 folder.
2. Navigate to the Initial Scene and **Double-Click** the actor named "Input" to open its Editor.
3. Add an empty Rule to the Behaviors window.
4. In this rule you'll need to build a condition that will accept keyboard input. To do this, **Choose** "key" from the second drop-down menu that currently reads "mouse position."
5. After selecting "key," a new input box will appear with a "Keyboard" button. **Press** this button and an image of a keyboard will open on-screen. From this image, **Click** on the "right" arrow key in the bottom right corner of the Keyboard window (see Figure 10.1).

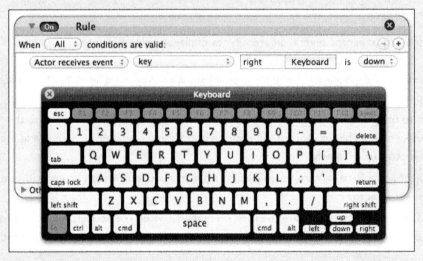

FIGURE 10.1
The keyboard input window.

6. The condition for the rule should now read:
   Actor receives event » key » right Keyboard » is » down

7. Nest a Move Behavior in the Rule.

8. Leave the Move Behavior's default values as they are.

9. Make a copy of this rule by selecting it and by choosing **Copy** from the **Edit** Menu.

10. Choose **Paste** from the **Edit** Menu to add the copy of the rule to the behaviors list.

11. In the copied version of the rule, update the condition to read:
    Actor receives event » key » left Keyboard » is » down

12. Update this rule's nested Move Behavior with a Direction of 180.

Note: Keyboard Values

When entering values in the keyboard input box, do not type in the word or letter for the keys. Press the keyboard button and click the appropriate key on the keyboard image.

Preview the scene and **Press** the Left and Right Arrow Keys on your keyboard. You'll see the square actor move sideways on-screen as long as you are holding one of the arrow keys down. When you release the key, the actor stops moving.

Tip: Video Game Logic

Video games can only do exactly what you tell them to do. If you try pressing any key besides the right and left arrow keys, nothing will happen. If you wanted the up and down arrow keys to move the actor up and down, you will need to add more rules to allow that to happen.

Mouse Input

Mice are often used to control video games; their button presses can be used for selecting menu options or units in a game. The position of the mouse pointer itself can be used to move game elements on-screen. Let's examine two types of mouse control, touch and click.

Exercise 10

Reading Mouse Input

In this exercise, you'll build some rules that will allow mouse position and button state controls.

1. Delete the two rules from the previous exercise so the Actor Behavior area is empty.

2. Add a new Rule and create a condition that reads:
    Actor receives event » mouse position » is » inside

3. Nest a Rotate Behavior in this rule and change its Speed to 200.

4. Make a copy of this rule and change the condition to read:
    Actor receives event » mouse button » is » down

5. Delete the Rotate Behavior and nest a Display Text behavior in its place.

6. In the Display Text Behavior, delete the text that reads "Hello world!" and type the word "Click!" You don't need to type the quotation marks.

7. **Click** the color box next to the Color Option in the Display Text Behavior and choose any color other than white.

8. Close the color picker once you have picked a color.

When you **Preview** this, it will seem that nothing happens. But when you move the mouse pointer over the square actor, it will begin to rotate. When you press the mouse button (anywhere on the stage), the word "Click!" will appear in the square.

Note: Independence

Since two different rules were added to the actor and each rule has its own set of conditions and actions, the actions independently take place from each other. Using the controls, you are able to make the actor rotate OR display text and rotate AND display text, depending on the actions of the mouse.

Touch Controls

Mobile devices are usually controlled by touch. The screens of these devices can detect where and when they have been touched. Gamesalad is able to detect up to eleven screen touches at one time. In addition to locating where an on-screen a touch occurs, Gamesalad is able to detect when the screen is touched and released and as well as if the touch is inside or outside a given actor.

Exercise 11

Touch Controls

In this exercise, you'll make the square actor react when it is touched.

1. Delete all of the Behaviors that are in the square actor from the previous exercise.
2. Add a new Rule to the actor and establish a condition that reads:
    Actor receives event » touch » is » pressed
3. Nest a Change Size Behavior in this rule and leave the Growth Rate as the default value of 1 (see Figure 10.2).

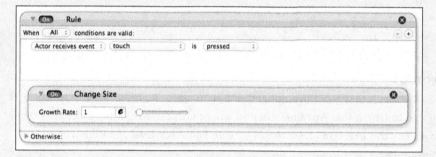

FIGURE 10.2
A rule that will trigger a touch event on a mobile device.

4. **Preview** the scene and note that when you click the mouse button (simulate a touch) on the actor, it will enlarge. Releasing the mouse button (touch) will cause the actor to stop growing.
5. Return to the actor editor and make a copy of the current rule. Change this rule's condition to read:
    Actor receives event » touch » is » outside
6. Update the Growth Rate of the Change Size behavior to -1.
7. This time, when you **Preview** the scene and touch inside the actor, it will grow. If you touch outside the actor, the actor will shrink.

Note: Multi-Touch Input
When testing games using touch controls on a desktop computer, Gamesalad will treat mouse clicks as though they are finger touches. This way you are able to playtest the game on your computer before exporting it for play on a mobile device.

Text Input

There are many times that players may need to input text into a game. For example, when they are creating a character in a role-playing game (RPG), they may be prompted to enter a name for the character.

Note: Prompting the Player

A prompt is when the computer or mobile device asks the player for some form of input. In this case, the game is asking the players to enter a text string.

Gamesalad has a special behavior specifically dedicated to creating a text input box for the player, the "keyboard input" behavior.

Exercise 12

Input Text Prompt

In this exercise, you'll create a text input prompt and display its contents on-screen. To accept text input, you are required to have a Text Attribute created where Gamesalad can store the text that is entered by the player. For this exercise I have already created an actor level attribute named "textInput" for this purpose.

1. Open the project file named "Text-Input" that is located in the asset files for Chapter 10 folder.
2. Go to the Initial Scene and open the input actor editor by **Double-Clicking** the actor. You'll see there is already a Display Text behavior included in the actor. You can leave this behavior as is.
3. Add a Rule to the list and create a condition that reads:
   Actor receives event » touch » is » pressed
4. Nest a Keyboard Input behavior in this rule. **Click** the (...) button next to the Change Attribute input box to open the Attribute Browser.
5. In the Attribute Browser, choose input in the first column and **Double-Click** "textInput" in the second column. The attribute "textInput" is a custom text attribute that has already been added to the actor for you.
6. In the input box next to Keyboard prompt, type the text "Please enter your name." This field acts as the title bar for the input box Gamesalad will display on- screen. The behaviors should look like Figure 10.3:

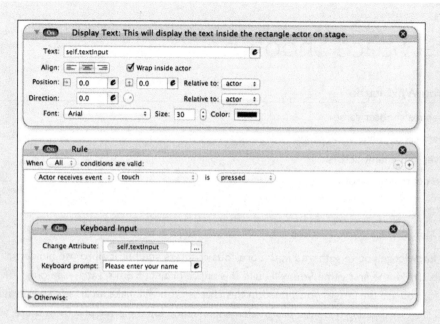

FIGURE 10.3
The completed text input behaviors.

7. **Preview** the scene and **Click** the white rectangle. The screen will fill with the text input prompt. Its title, created using the Keyboard prompt field, will be displayed within the title bar.

8. **Enter** some text in the input box and **Click** the **Done** button when you are finished.

9. The text you entered will now be displayed in the actor.

Note: Mobile Text Input

When the player is prompted for text input on a mobile device, the systems default on-screen keyboard will be displayed and used to accept the input.

Summary

In this chapter, you learned about the five ways Gamesalad is able to accept input, through the keyboard and mouse, with touch and accelerometer input on mobile devices and also by entering text. You started by learning how to build movement controls using the keyboard. Next, you learned how to control an actor by using mouse controls. You also learned how to add touch controls to a project and how Gamesalad uses mouse clicks to emulate touch controls while playtesting mobile games on a desktop computer. Finally, you learned how to add a text input prompt to a game.

er 11
e 2 – Space Shooter

In This Chapter You Will Learn:

» How to design a space shooter game

» How to build a parallax scrolling background

» How to build player and enemy actors

» How to add game control behaviors

It's time to use the knowledge you've gathered in the previous chapters and put it all to use building a fully functional game. Unlike the first game, you will build this entire project from scratch–the only elements provided for you are the images you'll need. In this chapter, you will make an arcade style space shooter game. You'll start by creating the basic design elements needed for the game and from there, you'll build all of the scenery and gameplay actors. You will include a game control actor that will dictate the enemy's frequency and finally, you will add a GUI actor to display the game's score for the player.

Note: Project Files
In case you get stuck, the starter project file and a finished version of the space shooter game can be found in the assets for Chapter 11 folder.

Game Concept

The first step in designing a game is to figure out what its concept is. For this space shooter, you will create an arcade style video game that could have been found in any video arcade during the 1980's. In this game, you will control a space ship that is flying over an alien planet. This space ship will battle alien ships that fly toward it from the right hand side of the screen. The player will score points by shooting and blasting the alien ships out of the sky.

Game Rules

The rules that will direct the space shooter game are:

» The player ship will start on the left side of the screen.
» Two kinds of enemies will fly toward the player at different speeds from the right side of the screen.
» The game is over when the player is destroyed.
» The player is able to shoot the enemies.
» Certain enemies are able to shoot at the player.
» The player is not able to leave the scene and will only be able to fly about halfway across the screen to the right.

Game Requirements

This game will require several graphic elements that have been provided for you in the starter file. In addition, you will be creating all of the behaviors needed to make the game playable. The requirements for the space shooter are:

» This game will be built to play in the Gamesalad Arcade.

Elements needed for the game include:

» 3 actors to create a parallax scrolling background.
» 1 actor for the player's spaceship.
» 2 enemy actors.
» Bullets for the player and the enemies.
» A game controller actor.
» A GUI score display.

Note: Parallax Scrolling
Parallax scrolling is a technique that is often used in video games that grew out of its use in traditional cell-based animation. This technique adds a feeling of depth to a game by scrolling background images at different speeds.

The Alien Planet

You'll begin creating the game by setting up the environment the action will take place in. This setting will be created using only three actors, but the way these actors are combined will give the game a lot of depth and life.

Before you begin creating the alien planet, make sure you have opened the starter file provided for this hour.

1. Since the background of this game will scroll, the first thing to do is navigate to the Initial Scene and turn on Wrap X in the Scene tab (see Figure 11.1).

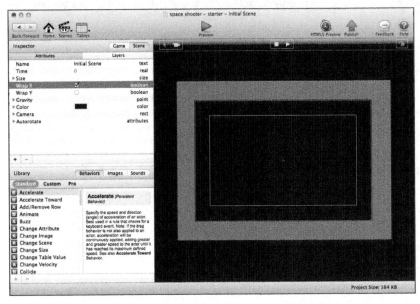

FIGURE 11.1
The Scene Attributes Tab with Wrap X active.

2. Return to the Game tab and find the image named "background-sky" in the Images tab of the Library Palette. **Drag** this image to the Actors tab in the Inspector Palette to create a new actor.

3. **Double-Click** the new background-sky actor and navigate to the Physics options. Now disable the Movable option (by unchecking it).

4. Return to the Stage and drag the background-sky actor onto the Stage. **Double-Click** the actor on the Stage and change its Positions to (240,160)–this will center the actor on the Stage.

Note: Movable

It is a good idea to always turn off the movable option if you are sure an actor will never move during a game. This lets Gamesalad know it can ignore the actor during some calculations and this can help reduce performance issues in some games.

5.   Next, **Drag** the image named "background-2" from the Library Palette to the Inspector Palette to create another actor.

6.   Now, place this new actor onto the Stage and change its Positions to (240,93).

7.   To create the final actor for the alien planet, create an actor from the image named "background-1."

8.   Place this actor on the Stage and change its Positions to (240,68). Your scene should now look exactly like Figure 11.2.

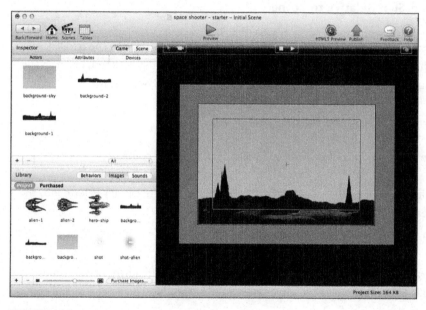

FIGURE 11.2
The completed alien background.

Animation

The background is now built, but it seems rather plain. It would be a lot more impressive if it were moving, adding some depth and realism to the game. The next step is to animate the layers of the background to make it come to life!

1. **Double-Click** the background-1 actor in the Library Palette. Make sure you are editing the Prototype Actor from the Library Palette and NOT the Instance Actor on the Stage.
2. Next, add a Move Behavior to this actor and set it up like this:
    Direction: 180 » Speed 75 » Relative to: scene

Note: Behavior Settings

For the rest of this book, if a specific setting in a behavior is not mentioned, it should be left at its default value. For example, the move type: should remain as additive in the move behavior you created in step 2.

---

3. Return to the Scene Editor and **Double-Click** the background-2 actor in the Inspector Palette.
4. Add a Move Behavior to this actor as well and set it up like so:
    Direction: 180 » Speed: 50 » Relative to: scene

Now, **Preview** the scene and you'll see the background scroll from the right to the left. The parallax effect is accomplished by setting the move speed of the foreground actor faster than the background actor. The darker color of the background actor also adds to the depth effect of the parallax scrolling.

The Player

In this section, you'll add the player's ship to the world and build its basic set of controls.

1. To create the player's alter ego, **Drag** the image named "hero-ship" from the Library Palette into the Inspector Palette to create an actor.
2. Place this new actor on the far left side of the Stage.

If you were to preview the game now, the hero ship will actually appear to be already flying since the background scrolls continually. However, to give the player control over the ship, you'll need to add some keyboard controls to the hero-ship actor.

1. **Double-Click** the hero-ship actor to open its Actor Editor and add an empty Rule to its list of behaviors.
2. Create a condition in this rule that reads:
    Actor receives event » key » up Keyboard » is » down
3. Then nest a Move Behavior in the rule and set its values as:
    Direction: 90 » Speed: 150 » Relative to: scene
4. Rename this Rule "Move Up" (see Figure 11.3).

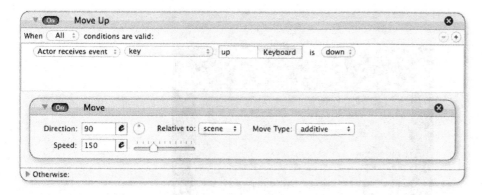

FIGURE 11.3
The completed 'move up' rule in the 'hero-ship' actor.

5. Make a copy of this Rule and name it "Move Down."
6. Change the Condition of the Rule to read:
    Actor receives event » key » down Keyboard » is » down
7. Change the Direction value in the Move Behavior to **270**.
8. Copy the Move Down Rule and change its name to Move Right.
9. In this Move Right Rule, change the key press of the condition to **Right** and the Direction of the Move Behavior to **0**.
10. Finally, make a copy of the Move Right Rule and change the name to Move Left. Update the key press of the condition to be **Left** and the Direction of the Move Behavior to be **180**.

Now **Preview** the game and you will have complete control over the players space ship. Using the arrow keys on they keyboard, you can freely move the ship up, down, left, and right. However, as you fly around, you might notice a few things that should be considered as errors. The spaceship can completely move off the screen at the top and bottom, it will wrap around to the right and left sides (since Wrap X is active in the Scene Settings), it can move too far to the right, and the ship also passes over (is on top of) both of the images used for the background landscape. Let's fix these "errors."

To correct the layering of the actors so the ship appears to fly between the layers of the background, navigate to the scenes Layers tab in the Inspector Palette. **Click** the arrow next to the Background Layer to expose the list of actors used on that layer (see Figure 11.4). Reorder the layers by dragging the hero-ship between background-1 and background-2 and release it.

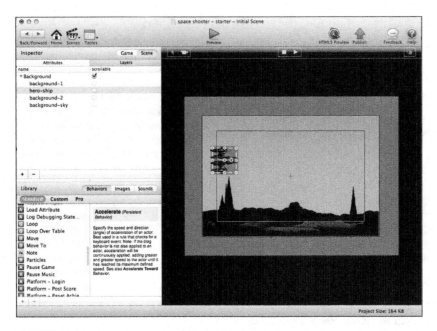

FIGURE 11.4
The 'hero-ship' actor has been placed between the two background actors in the Layers tab.

Preview the scene again. Now the player's ship will pass between the foreground and background layers of the planet.

Next, **Double-Click** the hero-ship actor and you'll learn how to limit the player movement on-screen by adding a second condition to each of the move rules that were created in the previous steps.

1. In the Move Up Rule, **Click** the **Plus (+)** button to add a second condition. Create this condition to read:
    Attribute » self.Position.Y » less than or equal to (≤) » 300

2. In the Move Down Rule, add a second condition that reads:
    Attribute » self.Position.Y » greater than or equal to (≥) » 75

3. In the Move Right Rule, create a second condition that reads:
    Attribute » self.Position.X » less than or equal to (≤) » 150

4. In the Move Left Rule, add a second condition that reads:
    Attribute » self.Position.X » greater than or equal to (≥) » 40

Note: Attribute Browser

Remember, you'll need to use the Attribute Browser to access the Actor Attributes (see Figure 11.5).

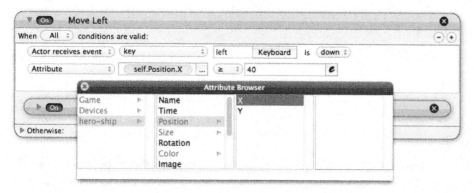

FIGURE 11.5
Using the Attribute Browser to create a second Condition in the Move Left Rule.

Preview the scene and you'll see the ship now has freedom of motion, but only within a set of limited X- and Y-coordinates. All this movement is great, but since this game is being created as an arcade space shooter, you'll need to add the ability for the player to shoot next.

Before you can add the actual behaviors to the hero-ship actor to allow shooting, you'll need to create the actor that will be shot from the ship. Create this new actor by **Dragging** the image named "shot" (it looks like a yellow dot) into the Inspector Palette. Open the shot actor editor. Add a Move Behavior and change the Relative to: option to scene.

Next, return to the Actor Editor for the hero-ship and:

1. Add a new Rule and create a condition that reads:
   Actor received event » key » space Keyboard » is » down
2. Nest a Spawn Actor Behavior in this rule and choose these options:
   Actor: shot » Layer Order: in back of actor » Position x: 36 (see Figure 11.6)
3. Rename this Rule "Shoot."

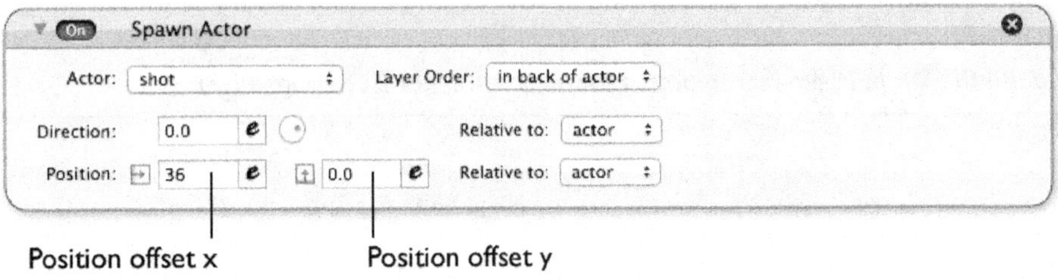

Position offset x   Position offset y

FIGURE 11.6
The Spawn Actor Behavior.

Note: Position Offsets

Remember that the origin point of every actor is its center. When one actor spawns another, it spawns the new actor from its own center point by default. You can use the Position Offsets (x,y) to change the location from which the new actor is spawned. For example, by using an X Position of 36, you told the shot to spawn from the front of the hero-ship actor instead of its center point.

Preview the scene and test the shot by pressing the space bar—the shot should shoot out of the front of the ship and fly across the screen to the right. But since Wrap X is active, the bullet wraps from the right side of the screen and travels back to the left. This can be fixed by adding another rule to the shot actor. Create this rule like so:

1. Open the shot Actor Editor and add a Rule to its behavior list.
2. Establish a condition that reads:
    Attribute » self.Position.X » greater than or equal to (≥) » 470
3. Nest a Destroy Behavior in this rule and name the rule "Destroy the shot."

Now, when you shoot a bullet, they will not wrap around the edge of the screen because Gamesalad destroys them once their X Position is greater than or equal to 470.

Tip: Independent Actor Behaviors

The player's shot is a good example of how behaviors act independently of each actor. Through a combination of including the move behavior in the shot actor and then spawning the shot actor with the shoot rule in the hero-ship, the shot actor will be dynamically added to the scene. Once spawned, its own behaviors will take control of it and move it across the screen.

Aliens
Alien 1

In any good space shooter, you need a few aliens to use for target practice. Follow the steps below to add two aliens to the game.

Tip: Plan Your Behaviors

As your games become more complex, you should take a moment before adding behaviors to each actor and plan the action that each actor will need to perform. The aliens in this game will be set up to appear on the right side of the screen. They will fly to the left and disappear if they reach the left edge of the screen. The aliens will also need to be destroyed if they are hit by the player's shot or if they collide with the player's ship.

---

1. Create a new actor using the image named "alien-1" and **Double-Click** to open its editor.
2. To make the ship fade in when it appears on-screen, add an Interpolate Behavior and set it up to read:
    Interpolate Attribute: self.Color.Alpha » to: 1» Duration: 0.1
3. Next, change the value of the alien-1 actors Alpha Attribute from 1 to 0. This is located under the Color Attributes in the actor Attributes Editor.

Note: Invisibility

When an actor's alpha value is changed to 0, the preview image of the actor will disappear. Don't worry, the image is not gone, it has just been made invisible.

---

4. To make the actor move across the screen once it has appeared, add a Move Behavior to the list and set it up to read:
    Direction: 180 » Speed: 100 » Relative to: scene
5. Now add a Rule that will destroy the enemy when it is hit by the player's shot. Set this rule's condition to read:
    Actor receives event » overlaps or collides » with » actor of type » shot
6. Nest a Destroy Behavior in this rule and name this Rule "Shot by player."
7. Copy this Rule and rename it "Hit the player" and update this rule's condition to read:
    Actor receives event » overlaps or collides » with » actor of type » hero-ship
8. Finally, add a new rule and name it "Phase Out" with a condition that reads:
    Attribute » self.Postiion.X » less than or equal to (≤) » 40
9. Nest an Interpolate Behavior in this rule and change its default values to read:
    Interpolate Attribute: self.Color.Alpha » Duration: 0.1

10. Nest a Timer Behavior below the Interpolate Behavior and set it up to read:
   After 0.1 seconds » Run to Completion should be checked
11. Nest a Destroy Behavior in the Timer Behavior.

Tip: Bug Hunting

As rules get more complex, it becomes easier to make a mistake or create a bug in the behaviors. When playtesting this game, if things don't work as expected, remember there is a completed version included with the files for this book. If need be, you can troubleshoot the project by using that version to compare the behaviors you create to a set of working behaviors.

Note: Phasing Out

The phase out rule uses an interpolate behavior in conjunction with a timer behavior. Take a close look and you'll see that the duration of the interpolate matches the time in the timer behavior. This will cause the image of the actor to fade out during a time span of .1 seconds. Once those .1 seconds pass, the timer will trigger and delete the actual actor from the scene.

Alien 2

Now that you have spent all that time making the first alien, it would be a real pain to have to repeat the whole process for the second alien. You won't have to do that though! All you have to do is make a copy of the first alien actor (in the actors tab of the inspector palette) and rename it "alien-2." Open this new "alien-2" actor and **Drag** the image named "alien-2" into the preview image. Since the preview image is already invisible, you won't see a change, but when this actor shows up on stage, it will have the new image in place.

The only other change you'll need to make to alien-2 is to make it move faster than alien-1. To do this, open the Move Behavior of alien-2 and update the Speed setting to **150**. Everything else can remain the same as alien-1.

Most of the work on the aliens is complete now, but they still won't appear on-screen. In order to get them to show up throughout the game, you'll need to set up and use a game controller.

The Game Controller

It is common to create a separate actor to act as a game controller; however, it's also possible to use any existing actor in the game as the control actor. As long as the control actor is ALWAYS on-screen, it can be any actor you choose. In this game, you will use the actor named "background-2" as the controller. The main reason to choose this actor is because, like the hero-ship, the aliens should fly between the layers of the background images. By using background-2 as the controller, the aliens' ships can be spawned between the two background layers easily.

1.   Open the Actor Editor for background-2 and add a Timer Behavior. Name this behavior "Timer: Spawn Alien Ship 1."

2.   Set this Timer up to read:
     Every random(1,3) » with Run to Completion checked

Don't type in the word "random." Instead, **Click** the **Expression Editor (e)** button next to the seconds field. Choose the Random Function from the Insert Function menu (see Figure 11.7) and replace the words "min,max" with "1,3." **Click** the green check mark to close the Expression Editor.

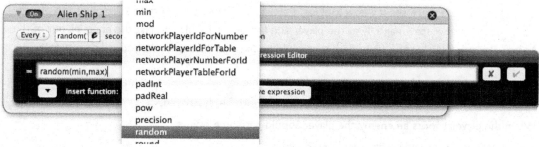

FIGURE 11.7
Choosing the Random Function in the Expression Editor.

Note: Functions
Functions are special mathematical formulas that can be accessed when using the Expression Editor. In a later chapter, the expression editor will be looked at in more detail.

---

3.   Nest a Spawn Actor Behavior in this Timer and set its values to:
     Actor: alien-1 » Layer Order: in front of actor » Position x: 445 » Position y: random(65,250) » Relative to: scene (See Figure 11.8)

FIGURE 11.8
The completed rule used to spawn Alien Ship 1.

4. Next, make a copy of this Timer Behavior and rename it "Timer: Spawn Alien Ship 2."

5. Finally, make the updates below and the controller will be complete.

    In the Timer Behavior:

    Every: random(2,6)

    In the Spawn Actor Behavior:

    Actor: alien-2

Preview the game and you'll see it's now looking pretty good. In addition to the background and player actors, the enemies now spawn and fly at the player and the player is able to blast the enemies out of the sky! As you play, you'll likely see a few things that could be fixed, added, or made better. For example:

1. The player's shot should disappear when it destroys an enemy.
2. When the player collides with an enemy, they should both be destroyed.
3. When the player shoots an enemy, the player should get some points.
4. The points scored should be displayed on-screen.
5. The enemies should be allowed to shoot back at the player.

Game Extras

All of the items outlined above are pretty easy to add; let's start at the top and destroy the player's shot when it hits an enemy. Since there are two aliens, the bullet will need to be removed from the scene when it collides with either enemy. The best way to deal with collisions that can occur with two or more actors is to create a tag set. A tag set is comprised of actors that are "grouped" together using an identifier Gamesalad calls a "tag."

1. Navigate to the Home Screen. From there, **Click** on the Actors Tab and **Click** the **Plus (+)** button in the lower left corner of the screen to add a new tag. Name this tag "Aliens" (see Figure 11.9).

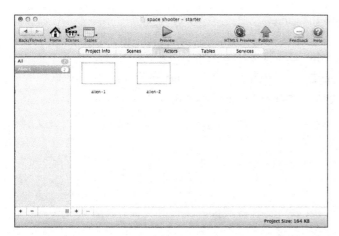

FIGURE 11.9
The actors alien-1 and alien-2 added to the Aliens Tag.

2. After creating the Aliens Tag, **Click** on the "All" tag at the top of the list and **Drag** the two alien actors onto the Aliens Tag title. When the title highlights, release the actors and they will be included in the tag set.

3. Next, navigate to the Actor Editor for the shot actor and add a Rule to the behaviors list. Create a condition for the rule that reads:
   Actor receives event » overlaps or collides » with » actor with tag » Aliens

4. Finally, nest a Destroy Behavior in this rule.

5. To make the next step super quick and easy, **Copy** the rule you just created.

6. Next, you will set up the hero-ship to be destroyed if the player collides with an alien. Open the Actor Editor of the hero-ship and **Paste** the rule you copied from the shot actor into the Behavior list. This rule is already set up to destroy the actor when it collides with either of the alien ships, so you don't have to make any edits to it.

The first step in creating a score system for the game is to add a custom game level attribute that will be used to keep track of the score.

1. Navigate to the Attributes Tab of the Inspector Palette.

2. **Click** the **Plus (+)** button in the lower left corner of the palette.

3. Choose integer as the attribute type and name the attribute "score."

4. Leave the default value as 0.

The next step is to actually add scorekeeping to the game.

1.   Open the Actor Editor of alien-1 and open the rule named "Shot by player."
2.   Nest a Change Attribute Behavior *above* the Destroy Behavior in this rule and set it up to read:
     Change Attribute: game.score » To: game.score+10 (see Figure 11.10).

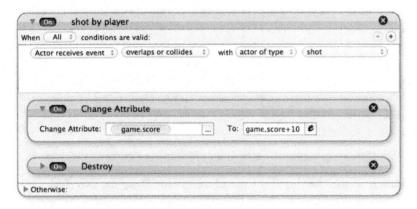

FIGURE 11.10
The updated 'shot by player' rule with scorekeeping added.

3.   **Copy** this Change Attribute Behavior and **Paste** it into the "Shot by player" rule of the alien-2 actor. Make sure it is pasted *above* the Destroy Behavior.

The score will now be calculated while the game is being played, but it is not being shown to the player yet. That is easy to fix:

1.   Add a new empty actor to the Actors Tab and open its Actor Editor. This actor will not have an image; it will act as a Graphical User Interface (GUI) object and display the score on-screen.
2.   Open the new actor's Attributes Editor and change the Red, Green, and Blue settings under Color to **0** and Alpha to **0.5**. Turn Moveable **Off** under the Physics settings as well.
3.   Add a Display Text Behavior and open the Expression Editor by **Clicking** the **(e)** button. In the Expression Editor, choose game.score as the Text value.
4.   Set the rest of the Display Text Behaviors options to read:
     Align: Center » Font: Helvetica Neue » Size:14 (See Figure 11.11)

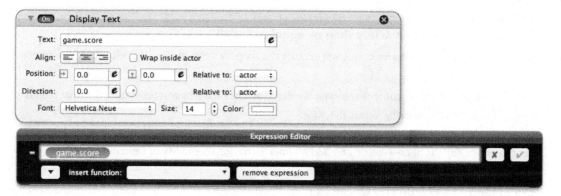

FIGURE 11.11
The completed Display Text Behavior for the on-screen GUI.

5. Finally, name this actor "display-score" and place it on the stage. **Double-Click** the actor to open its Editor and update these attributes:
    Positions (240,305) » Sizes (480,30)

Preview the game and you'll see the score is being properly kept and displayed across the top of the stage.

Finally, to be fair, we should give one of the alien ships the ability to shoot at the player.

1. First create a new actor using the image named 'shot-alien'.
2. Before adding any behaviors to the actor, navigate to the Actors Tab from the Home screen. Once there, **Drag** the newly added shot-alien actor into the Tag named Aliens. Once added to the tag group, the shot-alien actor will automatically destroy the players ship when they collide.
3. Open the Actor Editor for the shot-alien actor.
4. Add a Move Behavior to the Behaviors list and set it up to read:
    Direction: 180 » Relative to: scene
5. Add a Rule to the list and create two conditions that read:
    Actor receives event » overlaps or collides » with » actor of type » hero-ship
    Actor receives event » overlaps or collides » with » actor of type » shot
6. In this Rule make sure you set up the top menu to read:
    When Any conditions are valid:
7. Nest a Destroy Behavior in the Rule. This rule will destory the aliens shot if it collides with the player or the players shot.

8. Create another empty Rule and create its condition to read:
    Attribute » self.Position.X » less than or equal to (≤) 10

9. Nest a Destroy Behavior in this Rule. This will destroy the alien shot if it reaches the left side of the screen.

Now that all of the behaviors to control and destroy the alien shot have been completed, the final step is to allow one of the aliens to actually shoot the shot.

1. Open the editor for the alien-1 actor and add a Timer Behavior to the list of Behaviors.

2. Set the Timer Behavior up to read:
    Every random(1,3) seconds » Check Run to Completion

3. Nest a Spawn Actor Behavior in the Timer and set it up to read:
    Actor: shot-alien » Layer Order: in back of actor » Position x: -32

Preview the game now and the first alien actor should periodically shoot at the player.

Improving the Battle

Even though this space shooter is now a complete game, it certainly could be made even better. It's always worth asking yourself "how could I make this game better and what could I add or change?" Don't be afraid to return to elements you have already added and try new and different things—just keep a back up copy of your past work in case you don't like what you've done and want to return to a previous version.

Summary

In this chapter, you created an arcade style space shooter game. You started by designing the game and planning out the game's rules and requirements. Then you created the actors and added a parallax scrolling background. You then added the player's on-screen alter ego and provided enemies for the player to blast. Finally, you added scoring and built a GUI so the player can keep track of the game's score.

Chapter 12
Audio

In This Chapter You Will Learn:

» What audio file formats Gamesalad supports

» How to add music to a game

» How to add sound effects to a game

In this chapter, you will learn about using audio in Gamesalad projects. You will learn what audio formats Gamesalad supports and how to add audio files to your projects. Next, you will learn about the audio specific behaviors you have access to when building games. Finally, you will experiment with audio in a working project.

Game Audio

As you can probably tell after completing the space shooter game from the previous chapter, audio adds a lot to the video game experience. Since there was no audio in that game, it really seemed to be lacking. Imagine how the sounds of lasers blasting and explosions going off could enhance the game. On top of that, add in a sound track of sci-fi techno music and the experience would seem so much richer and exciting. After completing this chapter, you'll have an understanding of how to use audio in your games to create that experience.

Audio Styles

Audio can be used for two general purposes in Gamesalad: music and sound effects. When importing a new audio file, you will be prompted to choose a style for how that audio will be used in the game.

» **Music Style:** This is best used for audio files that will play longer than 30 seconds. A good use for music style audio would be a background soundtrack to a game.

» **Sound Effect Style:** This is best used for short audio files that will be played repeatedly. A good use for sound effect style audio would be a "jump" sound that is played every time the player jumps.

Importing Audio

Importing audio into a Gamesalad project is done through the sounds tab in the library palette. To import an audio file located on your computer, press the plus (+) button in the lower left corner of the window (see Figure 12.1).

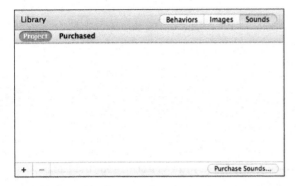

FIGURE 12.1
The Sounds Tab of the Library Palette.

In addition to importing audio files located on your computer, you can use the "purchase sounds..." button (in the lower right corner of the palette) to visit the Gamesalad Marketplace and purchase audio files.

Gamesalad supports the following audio formats:

» Audio Interchange File Format (.aiff)

» MPEG-1 Layer-3 Format (.mp3)

» Ogg Format (.ogg)

» Waveform Audio File Format (.wav)

When importing a new sound, you will be presented with the import sound dialog box (see Figure 12.2). Choose the sound's style here and the audio file will be added to this list of available options.

FIGURE 12.2
The import sounds dialog box.

Note: Audio Formats

Audio files can take up a lot of memory in a game, memory that might be better spent on graphics or animations. Typically, MP3 files are the smallest file format and are best for use in games.

After importing an audio file, you can easily test it in the sounds tab by clicking the play button that is added to the sounds icon. Press this play button to hear the sound. If the sound is long and you want to stop it from playing, press the stop button that replaces the play button while the sound is playing.

While this palette is very similar to the images palette, sounds from this tab will never be dragged into the actors tab of the inspector palette like images are. Audio is added to actors and events only through behaviors.

Audio Behaviors
Music

» **Play Music.** When using the play music behavior, you will be presented with a drop-down menu of music files that have been added to the project. Choose which piece of music to play from this list. There is also a check box to enable/disable looping of the music.

» **Pause Music.** There are no options with the pause music behavior. When it is triggered, any music currently playing will be paused. To restart the music, trigger a play music behavior and choose "Resume Current Music" from the top of the drop-down list of available music files.

Exercise 13

Playing Music

Imagine for a moment that you have just completed a fantastic game and now all you have to do is add background music to finish the project. To add music to a game:

1. Create a new project and navigate to the empty Initial Scene. The platform can be anything you choose.
2. **Click** the **Plus (+)** button to add a new sound to the Sounds Tab in the Library Palette.
3. Add the file named "Music.mp3" from the asset files for Chapter 12 folder.
4. Choose "Import As Music" from the Import Dialog Box.
5. Next, create a new actor in the Actors Tab and name it "Play Music".

6. Open this new actors editor and **Drag** a Play Music Behavior into its Behaviors list.

7. Choose "music" from the Sound drop-down menu and check the Loop option (Figure 12.3).

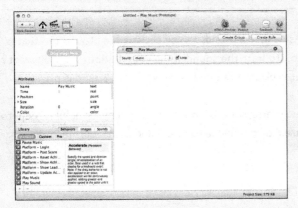

FIGURE 12.3
The Play Music Behavior added to the actor.

8. Finally, drag this actor onto the pasteboard, the light grey area, of the scene. Resize the actor as needed to keep it only on the pasteboard.

Preview the scene and you should hear the music play, but not see the actor. Since the actor is on the pasteboard, its behaviors function in the scene, but you won't see it because it is beyond the bounds of the live area of the scene.

Tip: Adding Behaviors

To quickly add any behavior to an actor, you can drag the behavior on top of the actor in the actors tab of the inspector palette. When you open the actors editor, you'll see the behavior already listed on its behavior list.

Sounds

» **Play Sound.** The play sound behavior offers more options than the play music behavior.

» **Sound:** Choose the sound to play from this drop-down menu.

» **Loop:** Enable the loop option to continually play the sound effect once it has been triggered.

» **Run to completion:** Enabling this option will force the entire sound effect to play from start to finish. There are instances when a sound effect will be nested in a timer or a rule that will try to "turn off" a sound effect before it has completed. Checking the "run to completion" option will force the entire sound effect to play regardless of what else is going on.

» **Volume:** Use the slider or enter a value to adjust the volume of the sound effect. A setting of 0 is no volume and a setting of 1 is full volume.

» **Pitch:** Use the slider or enter a value to adjust the Pitch of the sound effect. The sound's pitch can be adjusted with values of 0 – 10.

Tip: Pitch

Adjusting the pitch of a sound effect essentially speeds up or slows down the rate at which the sound plays, making it sound "higher" or "lower."

» **Positional Sounds:** This option will automatically adjust the volume of a sound based on the actor's location in the scene in relation to the camera. For example, if the sound emitting actor is placed on the right side of the stage, its sound will be louder from the right speaker and less loud from the left speaker.

» **Velocity Shift:** This will automatically adjust a sound's pitch based on its speed and direction. This option is only available when Positional Sound has been enabled.

Note: Volume

When playtesting a game, don't forget that the device determines the maximum volume level of the audio. If a sounds volume seems low, make sure the volume control on the device is turned up.

Exercise 14

Playing Sound Effects

In this exercise, you'll use three different sound effects to create a custom "wacky" keyboard.

1. First, create a new project and navigate to the Initial Scene. Again, this can be for any platform you choose.

2. Add to the Sounds Tab the three sound effect files; Coin.mp3, Keyboard.mp3, and Shot.mp3. These sounds are located in the asset files for Chapter 12 folder.

3. Choose "Import as Sound" in the Import Dialog Box. If you choose to import all three sounds at once, **Click** the "Apply to all" check box so this window only displays once.

4. Add an actor to the Actors Tab. Name it "Key 1" and open this actor's editor.

5. Add a Rule to the editor and create a condition that reads:
    Actor receives event » touch » is » pressed

6. **Drag** the Coin sound directly into this rule's Behaviors window. Gamesalad automatically nests a Play Sound Behavior for you and has the correct sound preselected in the drop-down menu.

7. Return to the Actors Tab and make two copies of they Key 1 actor, naming them "Key 2" and "Key 3."

8. Update the Play Sound Behavior of Key 2 by choosing Keyboard for the sound from the drop-down menu.

9. Update the Play Sound Behavior of Key 3 by choosing Shot for the sound from the drop-down menu.

10. Finally, add these three actors to the scene (see Figure 12.4).

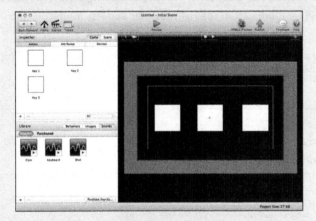

FIGURE 12.4
The sounds and 'keyboard' actors added to the stage.

Preview the scene and play the keys like they are keys on a piano. As you click each one, they will play their individual sounds.

Summary

In this chapter, you learned all about using audio in Gamesalad. You learned what audio formats can be imported for use as music and sound effects. Next, you learned what behaviors are used to play and pause music in a game and created a sample music project. You learned all about adding sound effects to a project as well as how to control the sound effects volume, pitch, and other settings. Finally, you created a sound effect keyboard using "wacky" sounds.

Chapter 13

The Expression Editor

In This Chapter You Will Learn:

» How to use the expression editor

» How to manipulate values using math functions

» How to manipulate text and text attributes using text functions

In this chapter, you will learn all about the expression editor—Gamesalad's tool for adding mathematic formulas to games. First, you'll learn how to open and navigate the expression editor and discover what options are available from within it. Next, you will learn how to add math functions to a game and learn what some of the most common math functions are used for. Then I will show you how to use text functions to manipulate text in your projects. Finally, you will use your knowledge of both math and text functions to work through a series of exercises using the expression editor.

Expression Editor Basics

The expression editor is available for use within many of Gamesalad's behaviors. Any time you see the "e" icon in a behavior, that icon can be clicked to expose the expression editor (see Figure 13.1).

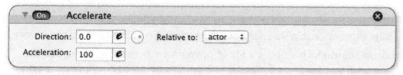

FIGURE 13.1
The Expression Editor can be opened by clicking on the "e" icon located next to an input box in behaviors.

From the expression editor, you have access to just about every editable setting Gamesalad has to offer. Open the expression editor from within a behavior so you can follow along or review Figure 13.2 below.

1. **Expression input box:** This input box is where you will create and edit the expression.
2. **Attributes arrow:** When clicked, this arrow will expose the attributes browser that is built into the expression editor. As you have already learned, this browser provides access to all of the attributes

used in a game. If the actor that is being edited is an unlocked instance actor, you will also have access to the scene attributes through this menu.

3. **Functions menu:** The insert function drop-down menu provides access to many mathematical, table, and text manipulation functions.

4. **Remove expression button:** Pressing this button will delete any expression that is currently displayed and will also close the editor.

5. **Accept button:** Pressing the green checkmark button will accept the expression and will also close the editor.

6. **Decline button:** Pressing red x button will cancel any edits that have been made to an expression and will also close the editor.

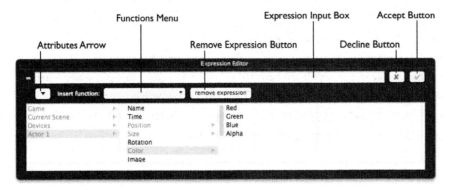

FIGURE 13.2
The Expression Editor .

Expressions created in the expression editor can be extremely simple or very complex; the complexity will depend on the specific use of the expression. Unlike most of Gamesalad, the expression editor is very open-ended and is not a drag and drop solution. This offers a lot of power when creating games, but can also be frustrating to learn. When creating a specific expression for a game, you will often have to employ trial and error to get the expected results. For more complex expressions, the best way to approach this is to first figure out what the expression should accomplish and then try different expressions to reach the desired goal.

Mathematical Expressions

While you can use the expression editor to manipulate text and tables, the most common use is certainly to perform math functions. The most basic of all the math functions are addition, subtraction, multiplication, division, and modulus. These are all accomplished by directly using the appropriate symbol in the expression (see arithmetic operators in chapter 6).

Exercise 15

Basic Math Function

In this exercise, you will create a simple expression that uses addition to manually move an actor 64 pixels to the right every time the actor is clicked on.

1. Create a new project for any platform and navigate to the Initial Scene.
2. Add an actor and change its size to **32x32** pixels.
3. Add a Rule to this actor and create a condition that reads:
   Actor receives event » touch » is » pressed
4. Nest a Change Attribute Behavior in the rule and choose **self.Position.X** from the Attributes Browser for the Change Attribute field.
5. Next, open the Expression Editor and **Click** the down arrow to expose the Attributes Browser. Choose **self.Position.X** and type "**+64**" (see Figure 13.3).

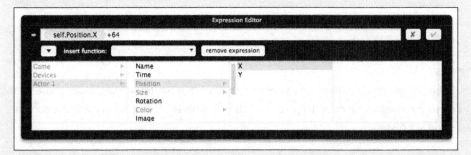

FIGURE 13.3
The completed expression in the Expression Editor.

6. **Press** Return and **Click** the green check mark to accept the expression and close the Expression Editor.
7. Navigate to the Stage and place the actor at the far left edge of the Stage.
8. Save this file. You'll use it again in the next exercise.

Preview the scene and you'll see that every time you click on the actor, it moves 64 pixels to the right.

Note: Order of Operations

Equations created in the expression editor follow the standard order of operations. Equations are evaluated from left to right, with multiplication and division being evaluated before addition and subtraction. Parentheses are used to evaluate certain parts of equations first.

In addition to the standard mathematical functions, you have access to a long list of built-in functions. Some of the most commonly used built-in functions are:

» **abs:** The abs function will return the absolute value (positive value) of a number or attribute. For example, abs(-4.97)=4.97.

» **ceil:** The ceiling function will round up a value to its nearest integer. For example, ceil(7.5)=8.

» **floor:** Using the floor function will round down a number to its nearest integer. For example, floor(2.2)=2.

» **max:** The maximum function will find the higher of two numbers. For example, max(50,82)=82

» **precision:** This will display a real number with the specified number of decimal places. The number of decimal places shown is determined by the second number (y) in the function. For example, prec(256.47983,2)=256.47.

» **random:** The random function will return a random number between the two values used in the function. For example, random(1,3) could return either 1, 2, or 3.

Exercise 16:

Randomness

Video games often rely on random numbers to help create a more natural feeling in the game. In this exercise, you'll use the random function to place an actor at different locations around the screen each time a button is pressed.

1. Begin with the file you finished in the last exercise and create a second actor in the Actors Tab.

2. Change this actor's size to 32x32 and change its color to anything other than white.

3. **Double-Click** the white square actor from the last exercise and delete the Change Attribute Behavior from the Rule.

4. Nest a Spawn Actor Behavior in this Rule and choose Actor 2 from the Actor drop-down menu.

5. Open the Expression Editor for the Position X input field (right arrow).

6. From the Insert Function menu, choose Random.

7. Delete the text between the parenthesis "min,max" and replace it with **0,game.Display Size.Width** (see Figure 13.4).

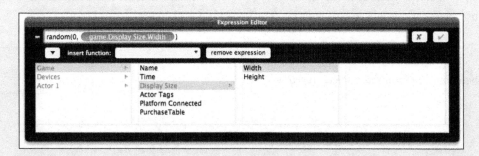

FIGURE 13.4
The completed expression for the Position X of the Spawn Behavior.

8. Open the Expression Editor for the Position Y input field (up arrow).

9. Add a Random function and set it up to read:
    random(0,game.Display Size.Height)

10. Choose **Scene** from the Positions Relative To menu.

Preview the scene and repeatedly **Click** on the white square actor. Each time you click, a new colored actor will appear in a random spot on the stage.

Tip: Screen Dimensions
Using the attributes "game.Display Size.Height" and "game.Display Size.Width" to determine the devices scene size is much more flexible than adding actual pixel values to behaviors. Using this method, it is possible to create games that will run on multiple devices regardless of their screen sizes.

Text Expressions

Text expressions are used to manipulate text and text attributes in a game, much the same way math functions are used with numbers. There are many uses for text and text manipulation. Text expressions can be used in conjunction with display text behaviors to write a score value in a games GUI or to display a list of high scores on a game over screen.

When entering text directly into the expression editor, the text must be surrounded with double quotation marks (e.g. "My Text"). Putting text inside quotation marks tells Gamesalad to treat it as text to be displayed on-screen and not evaluated as a formula.

The most common and simplest text expression is used to concatenate two, or more, text values. Gamesalad uses two periods in a row to indicate concatenation (..).

Note: Concatenation

Means to connect or link two or more objects together.

Excercise 17

Score Display

In this exercise, you will display a score value on-screen.

1. Start a new project for any platform type and navigate to the Initial Scene.
2. First, create a new Integer Attribute in the Attributes Tab and name it "**Score**". Give it a value of 100.
3. Create a new empty actor in the Actors Tab. Open the Actor Editor and change the value of Alpha to **0**. This will make the actor itself invisible, but *not* the text that it will display.
4. Add a Display Text Behavior to this actor and open the Expression Editor for the Text input field by **Clicking** the "e" icon to the right of the text field.
5. In this field, type (this time include the quotation marks): **"Score:"**..
6. With the cursor to the right of the two periods (..), **Click** the down arrow in the Expression Editor to expose the Attributes Browser and choose the Score Attribute that was just created from the Game list. The Display Text Behavior should look Figure 13.5:

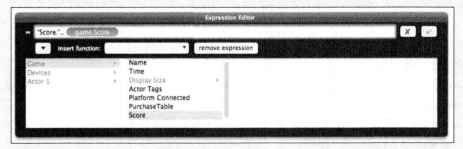

FIGURE 13.5
The completed expression for the Display Text Behavior.

7. Accept this expression and return to the Scene. Place the actor in the center of the Stage, and Preview the scene.

8. You should see the text "Score:100" displayed on-screen.

While that looks pretty good, it would look better if there was a space after the colon and before the number 100. To include a space in text that is entered in the Expression Editor, you'll need to use a special "escape character".

1. Return to the Display Text Behavior and open the Expression Editor.
2. Place the cursor between the colon and the quotation mark.
3. Type '\32' (without the quotation marks).
4. Accept the Expression and Preview the Scene.
5. Now the text will display as "Score: 100."

Escape Characters

There are certain characters that can't be directly entered in the Expression Editor; these characters must be input as special escape characters. Below is a list of common escape characters.

Table 13.1 Common Escape Characters

Character Code Entered	Character Output
\32	Space
\\	\
\"	"
\n	New Line
\r	Carriage Return

Text Functions

In addition to the math functions that were reviewed earlier in this chapter, Gamesalad offers a series of text functions as well. These functions are used to manipulate text and text attributes just like the math functions are used to manipulate numbers. Some of the most used text functions are:

» **textLength:** Using the textLength function will return the number of individual character in the text string. For example: textLength("Hello")=5.

» **textReplace:** This function is used to replace certain words or characters in a text string. The format of the function is textReplace(text,pattern,replacement).

   » **text:** Represents the source text to operate on.

   » **pattern:** Represents the word or character that will be replaced.

   » **replacement:** Represents the word used as a replacement.

   For example: textReplace("Hello World","Hello","Goodbye")=Goodbye World

» **textSubStr:** Use the textSubStr function when you need to separate some of the text from its surrounding characters. The format of the function is textSubStr(text,startIndex,endIndex).

   » **text:** Represents the source text to manipulate.

   » **startIndex:** Represents the number of the first character to separate.

   » **endIndex:** Represents the number of the last character to separate.

   For example: textSubStr("I Love Making Games",15,19)=Games

---

Note: Spaces and Escape Characters

Spaces and escape characters are counted as one character when using any of the text functions.

Additional Functions

The function menu also contains functions that can be used to manipulate tables, which will be examined in a later chapter. Networking functions are also listed, these are part of Gamesalad's implementation of multiplayer gaming and are a pro only feature.

Summary

In the last chapter, you learned the ins and outs of Gamesalad's Expression Editor. You learned how to use mathematical functions to manipulate attributes in your games. Next, you learned all about using text functions to control and work with text in projects. Finally, you experimented with some of the various math and text functions through a series of exercises.

Chapter 14
Collisions and Physics

In This Chapter You Will Learn:

» How to use collision detection

» What behaviors are used to control collisions

» What a collision shapes is

» How to control an actor's physical properties

In this chapter, you will learn how to control collisions between two or more actors and how to make those actors react to impact using physics. Gamesalad will detect collisions when the edge of one actor crosses the edge of another actor. After learning how to trigger a collision, you will learn to use the Gamesalad physics engine to control the actor's reactions. Finally, you'll experiment with various physics settings and learn how each one affects the actor's reactions during a collision.

Collisions

By default, actors created in Gamesalad are not set up to interact with each other. You must add the ability to collide with other actors while creating each actor's behaviors. There are two behaviors used to control collisions:

» **Collide:** When using the collide behavior, you'll use a drop-down menu to choose which actor type (or tag) the actor should collide with.

» **Rules:** Using a rule to control collisions requires creating at least one condition to trigger the rule's behaviors when the actor overlaps or collides with another actor type or tag.

Collision Shape

Each actor has a collision shape; this shape can either be a rectangle or a circle. The collision's shape for each actor can be changed within the physics settings in the actors editor (see Figure 14.1).

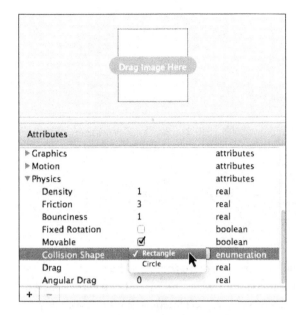

FIGURE 14.1
The two Collision Shape choices, Rectangle and Circle located within the Physics settings for each actor.

» **Rectangle:** Choosing a rectangle for the collision shape will use the physical outside edge of the actor as its collision shape (see Figure 14.2A).

» **Circle:** A circle collision shape is the largest circle that can be calculated within the actor's pixel dimensions, centered at the actor's origin (see Figure 14.2B).

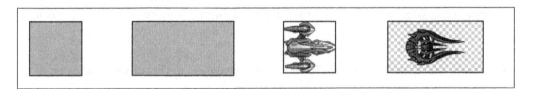

FIGURE 14.2A
Rectangular collision shapes as indicated by the box surrounding each image.

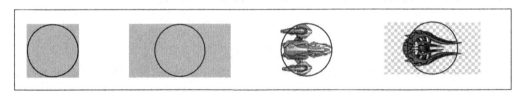

FIGURE 14.2B
Circular collision shapes as indicated by the circle within each image.

Note: Transparent Pixels

If the image used for an actor has "extra" transparent pixels beyond the visible edge of the image, those transparent pixels will be considered when Gamesalad calculates the collision shape for that actor. For this reason, images should be cropped to the exact edge of their visible pixels (see Figure 14.3).

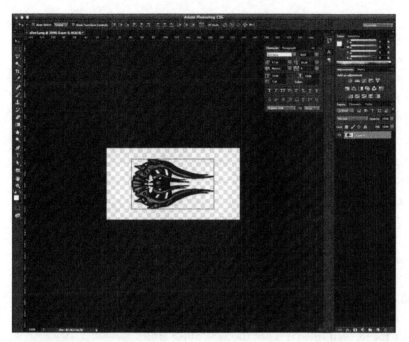

FIGURE 14.3
An actor image with surrounding transparent pixels in Adobe Photoshop. Instead of cropping to the far outside edge of the canvas, all images should be cropped at the edge of their visible pixels (as indicated by the surrounding box).

Physics

Gamesalad uses a version of the popular Box2d physics engine to simulate rigid body dynamics. By adjusting the physical properties of each actor in a game, you are able to control how the actors interact with each other during collisions. An actor's physical properties can be edited within the physics settings section of the actors editor (see Figure 14.1 above).

» **Density:** The density of an actor represents how heavy that actor is. A high value for density will make the actor heavier and more difficult to move by actors with a lower density setting. Density can be set to any real positive number. A density setting of 0 will make the actor immoveable by other actors in the game.

» **Friction:** Use the friction setting to control how much an actor slows down when it comes in contact with other actors. Large numbers will slow an actor more quickly while a setting of 0 will not slow an actor at all, making the actor smooth/slippery. Friction can be set to any real positive number.

» **Bounciness:** The bounciness setting literally describes how bouncy that actor will be. Bounciness can be set to any real number between 0 and 2, with 0 being not bouncy at all and 2 being very bouncy.

Note: It Takes Two (or More) to Tango

Most physics settings need to two or more actors to be in contact to have any effect in a game. When actors collide, both of the actors' physics settings are taken into consideration when displaying the results of the collision. For example, when a ball actor collides with a floor actor, both actors' bounciness settings will be used to calculate the height, speed, and distance of the ball's bounce.

» **Fixed Rotation:** Checking this box will "lock" an actor at its current rotation setting. An actor with fixed rotation will not change its rotation when it collides with other actors in the scene.

» **Moveable:** The moveable check box determines whether an actor can be moved in the scene. When this box is unchecked, the actor will not be moveable in the scene from collisions, gravity, or even most behaviors.

» **Collisions Shape:** Choose the actor's collision shape from this menu. As discussed in the previous section, you can choose either circular or rectangular.

» **Drag:** The drag setting is used to slow down an actor's movement in the scene. Higher numbers slow down actors more quickly. Drag can be set to any real positive number. Drag is similar to friction, but drag will always affect an actor's speed, even when it is not touching other actors.

» **Angular Drag:** The angular drag setting slows the rotation of an actor over time in the scene. Higher numbers will slow the rotation more quickly. Angular drag can be set to any real positive number.

Tip: Gravity

The gravity setting for each scene, available in the scene attributes settings tab, can be used in conjunction with the physics properties to affect all moveable objects in a scene.

The best way to understand how the various physics settings interact with each other is to test them out in a working project, which is exactly what you'll do in the next exercise.

Exercise 18

Physics Playground

In this exercise, you will create several scenes to test and play with the various physics settings Gamesalad offers.

Bounciness:

1. Open Gamesalad and start a new project. So you have a lot of room to play in, choose the iPad Landscape option for the platform. You can leave Resolution Independence turned off for this exercise.

2. Navigate to the Scene Attributes Tab of the Initial Scene and change the Gravity Y setting to **200**. This will apply a typical downward pull to all moveable actors placed in the scene.

3. Next, create two actors in the Actors Tab. Name the first actor "MainActor" and update its size to 50x50.

4. Name the second actor "Floor" and turn off (uncheck) Moveable, which is under the Physics settings options.

5. Return to the Stage and place the MainActor at the top center of the stage. Place the Floor actor at the bottom of the stage. Drag the width of the Floor actor so it fills the screen, side to side (see Figure 14.4)

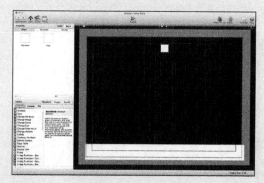

FIGURE 14.4
The Stage with the MainActor and Floor actors placed.

6. Open the actor editor of the MainActor and drag a collide behavior into its behaviors list. Set this behavior up to read:

   Bounce when colliding with: » actor of type » Floor

Preview the scene. The MainActor will now drop (due to the gravity setting) and bounce when it collides with the Floor. Because both actors have a bounciness setting of 1, the MainActor bounces back up to the top of the stage—in fact, if you let it bounce long enough, the height of the bounce will increase until it moves out of the stage's live area.

Try the variations below and watch how they change the interaction of the two actors. **Preview** after each alteration to view the changes. Remember the Bounciness setting is located under each actors Physics settings.

1. Reduce the bounciness setting of the Floor to **0**.
2. Reduce the bounciness of the MainActor to **.5**.
3. Reduce the bounciness of the MainActor to **0**.
4. Increase the bounciness of the Floor to **2**.

Friction:

1. Change the bounciness setting of the Floor actor to **0**.
2. Add another copy of the floor actor to the stage and change its rotation to **350°**. Change its size and update the placement of the new Floor actor and the MainActor to something like you see in Figure 14.5:

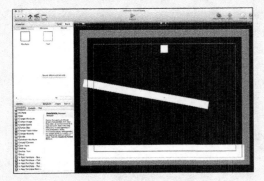

FIGURE 14.5
The Stage with the additional Floor actor placed.

3. Navigate to the Scene Attributes Tab and activate the Wrap X option.

Preview the scene. You should see the MainActor drop, hit the slanted floor, slide along it, drop to the bottom floor, and continue sliding. The MainActor should stop sliding once it has wrapped around the scene once.

Try these variations and **Preview** after each one:

1. Change the Friction setting of the Floor and MainActor to **0**.
2. Change the Friction of the Floor to **3** and the MainActor to **35**.

Fixed Rotation:

1. Increase the bounciness of the MainActor to **.8**.

Preview the scene and notice how the MainActor now bounces, spinning off the slanted floor until it eventually comes to a stop on the bottom floor.

Try this alteration:

1. Activate Fixed Rotation in the MainActor and **Preview** the scene.

Angular Drag:

1. Open the actor editor for the MainActor, turn off Fixed Rotation, and change Bounciness to **1**.
2. Change the Rotation of the slanted floor actor to **345°**.

Preview the scene and the MainActor should bounce and wildly spin all around the scene after it collides with the slanted floor.

Try these variations and **Previewing** after each one:

1. Change the Angular Drag of the MainActor to **2**.
2. Increase the Angular Drag of the MainActor to **50**.

Drag:

1. Update the physics settings of the MainActor to read:
    Friction: 1 » Bounciness: 0 » Angular Drag: 0

When you **Preview** the scene, it should look familiar. The MainActor drops and slides down the slanted floor to land and eventually stops on the bottom floor.

Try these alterations and **Preview** after each one:

1. Change the MainActor's Drag to **25**.
2. Increase the MainActor's Drag to **50**.
3. Increase the Drag setting of the MainActor to **175**.

Density:

1. Create a new actor named "Box" and set its physics to:
    Density 10 » Friction 100 » Bounciness 0.
2. Add a Collide Behavior to the Box actor and set it up to collide with the Floor actor.
3. Place a copy of the Box actor in the scene, just above the bottom third of the slanted floor (see Figure 14.6).

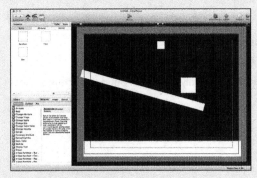

FIGURE 14.6
The Stage with the additional Box actor placed.

4. Open the MainActor's editor and add an additional Collide Behavior set to collide with the Box actor.
5. Update the MainActor's physics settings to:
    Density 1 » Friction 3 » Drag 0

Preview the Scene and note how the MainActor stops moving when it collides with the Box actor.

Try these variations and **Preview** after each one:

1. Change the Box actor's Density to **2**.
2. Increase the Density of the MainActor to **10**.

By working with the many physics settings Gamesalad offers, you can create any kind of interaction you can imagine between actors. You can create "real world" collisions, bouncing balls, slippery slopes, or sticky floors. You can even create "other worldly" gravity-defying interactions. The possibilities are truly only limited by your imagination.

Note: Relativity

Physical interactions do not need to be based on any real world values; the important thing to keep in mind is that all the values used should be relative to each other. For example, if you want to create one actor that is twice as bouncy as another, you can use bounciness values of .1 and .2 or .5 and 1. In both cases, the second actor will be twice as bouncy as the first.

Summary

During the last chapter, you learned about collision shapes and how to trigger collisions using them. Then you learned about all of the physics settings each actor has and what each setting controls. Finally, you created a "physics playground" project and experimented with many of the physics settings to get firsthand experience with how they affect actor interactions.

Chapter 15:
Camera Control and Graphical User Interfaces

In This Chapter You Will Learn:

» What the camera attributes control

» How to create a scrolling scene

» Graphical User Interface (GUI) basics

» How to create a GUI Layer

» How to create some common GUI elements

In this chapter, you will learn about Gamesalad's camera system and how to create an Graphical User Interface (GUI) to offer players important information about the game. You will begin by learning about the various camera settings and experiment with creating a scrolling scene where the camera automatically follows an actor. Next, you learn how to create a special GUI layer and use this layer to create the game's Graphical User Interface. Finally, you will learn about and create some common GUI elements.

The Camera

Every game created in Gamesalad can have only one active camera; this camera is the player's view of the game world. While a scene can be any size, a size much larger than a device's screen size, the camera size indicates the area of the scene that will be displayed on-screen (see Figure 15.1).

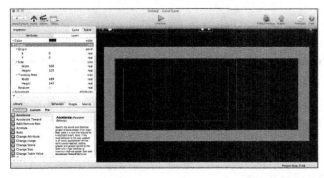

FIGURE 15.1
The Camera Attributes and Guidelines.

The camera has several attributes that can be manipulated during game play. The camera's attributes are:

» **Origin X, Y:** This is the starting position of the camera in a scene. The default starting location for the camera is (0,0).

» **Size (width, height):** These values set the width and height of the camera, indicating how much of a scene will be visible on-screen. The camera size is indicated by the outer white guideline shown on the stage.

» **Tracking Area (width, height):** This set of values determines the area within the camera view that will "snap to" or follow an actor that has a Control Camera Behavior applied to it. The camera tracking area is indicated by the inner white guideline shown on the stage.

» **Rotation:** The rotation of the camera.

By manipulating the camera's attributes, you are able to create things like camera panning, zooming, and rotating.

Tip: Panning

Panning is a term that is often used in photography and videography. Panning means to move a camera to the right or left. What the camera "sees" through its lens appears to move in the opposite direction. For example, panning the camera to the right results in the images in the camera's view to move toward the left.

Exercise 19

Camera Panning

Camera panning is often used in games. For example, in the popular game "Angry Birds," the camera pans to reveal the pig's fortress before the game begins. In this exercise, you will create a similar effect. Open the file named "Camera Pan" provided in the assets folder for Chapter 15. This starter project is created for the Gamesalad Arcade platform, which is 480x320 pixels. Note that the scene size is much larger; however, it has been set to 2048x640 pixels.

1. Begin by **Double-Clicking** the landscape actor that is already placed on the stage.
2. Unlock the actor to make it an instance actor. This step is needed to gain access to the Camera's Attributes that are located in the Scene Attributes.
3. Add a Rule and create a condition that reads:
    Actor receives event » mouse button » is » down

4. Nest an Interpolate Behavior in the Rule and set it up to read:
    Interpolate Attribute: scene.Camera.Origin.X » to » 1,568 » Duration » 3 (see Figure 15.2).

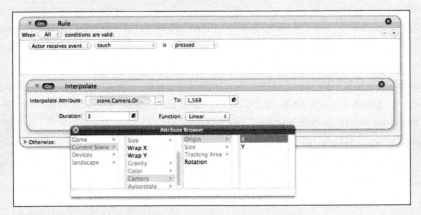

FIGURE 15.2
The completed pan Rule.

5. Open the Otherwise section of the Rule and add a copy of the Interpolate Behavior. Change the
    value of **1,568** back to **0**.

Preview the scene and hold the mouse button down. Keep the button pressed until the movement stops.
You'll see the background appears to move toward the left; however, what is actually happening is the camera
is panning toward the right. When you release the mouse button, the camera will pan back to its original
position.

Camera Tracking

The camera tracking area works in conjunction with the Control Camera Behavior. When a moving actor,
with a control camera behavior applied to it, reaches the edge of the camera tracking area, the camera will
automatically being to follow the actor.

There are two ways to edit the camera's tracking area. The width and height of the camera tracking
area can be directly edited in the Scene Attributes Tab or the interactive tracking editor can be used.
(see Figure 15.3).

Clicking the camera icon at the top left of the stage will reveal a yellow area on the stage and four handles;
these handles are used to increase or decrease the size of the tracking area. Also when in camera editor

mode, the camera origin can be changed by clicking anywhere within the white guidelines and dragging the camera zone to a new location on the stage.

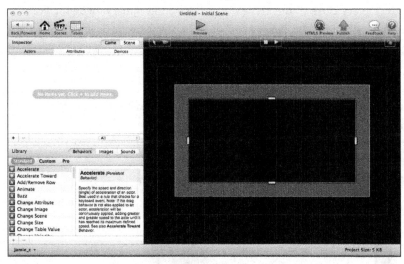

FIGURE 15.3
The Stage has been put into Camera Editor Mode.

Exercise 20

Camera Tracking

In this exercise, you will create a camera that tracks and actor as it moves around a large scene.

Start by opening the file named "Camera Scroll" from the asset folder of the files provided for Chapter 15. This file starts with a large scene (2048x640) already created.

Preview the scene and you'll see that the arrow keys on the keyboard can be used to freely move the space ship around the scene. However, once the ship reaches the edge of the scene, the ship can move out of the camera's view.

1. From the Stage Editor, **Double-Click** the hero-ship Actor to open its Actor Editor; you'll see there is a group of behaviors already included that control the Actor's movements.
2. Add a Control Camera Behavior to the list of behaviors. There are no options for this behavior; it just lets Gamesalad know that this is the actor the camera should automatically track.

Preview the scene. As the ship approaches the edge of the scene, the camera will follow it as it moves. However, the ship has to get very close to the scene's edge before the camera follows it. For this type of game, it would be more typical for the camera to follow the ship as soon as it starts to move. That change can quickly be made by adjusting the camera's tracking area.

1. Return to the scene and **Click** the camera editor icon.
2. Adjust both the horizontal and vertical handles of the camera tracking area so they are directly at the center of the stage (see Figure 15.4)

FIGURE 15.4
The Camera Tracking Zone adjusted to be closed on the center of the live area.

3. Save this project. You will use it again in the next section.

Preview the scene and the camera will now begin to follow the ship actor as soon as it beings to move.

Note: Control Camera

There can be only one active Control Camera Behavior in a scene at one time.

Tip: Scene Scrolling

A scene is only able to scroll in any given direction while there is more of the scene to display. If the scene runs out of information to display, the camera scrolling will automatically stop.

Graphical User Interface

A graphical user interface (GUI) is a special layer of your game that displays important information during game play and can also accept player input. GUI controls are built using actors and Gamesalad's standard behaviors.

Some common items that might be displayed in a GUI include:

» The game score

» A player's health

» An item in the player's possession

» Time left in the game

» Messages to the player

» Settings controls (i.e. sound volume)

» Buttons (i.e. pause button)

A GUI should be built on its own special layer in the layers tab (see Figure 15.5). By creating a separate layer for the GUI, you are able to easily identify its elements and keep the GUI stationary on-screen if the rest of your game scrolls.

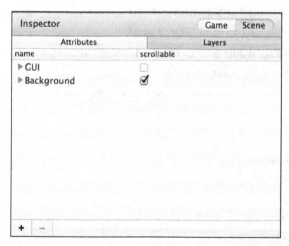

FIGURE 15.5
A special GUI layer has been created in the Scene Layers Palette.

GUI Elements

In the following section, you will learn to build some common GUI elements using Gamesalad's behaviors.

GUI Messages and Labels

To display a text message to the player, you will use a Display Text Behavior.

Note: GUI Exercises

All of the GUI exercises will use the scrolling camera project as a starting point. If you didn't save the project, return to the previous section and create and save the project.

Exercise 21

Text Label

In this exercise, you'll add a text label to the previous scrolling camera project.

1. Open the "Camera Scroll" project created in the pervious section and add a new actor to the project.

2. Name this actor "TextLabel." Open the actor editor and change its Alpha setting to **0**.

3. Add a Display Text Behavior and change the default text to read "**Text Label**."

4. Return to the scene and **Drag** this actor to the top/middle area of the scene. When you release it on the stage, it will be invisible since you set the alpha value to 0.

5. **Click** the actor and it will highlight. Change its size and placement to look something like Figure 15.6.

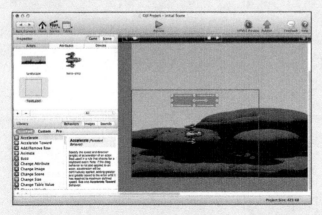

FIGURE 15.6
The TextLabel actor has been added to the Stage.

Preview the scene and it will display the words "Text Label" at the top/center of the screen. However, this will not work as a successful GUI just yet. Move the ship around the screen and you'll see the text scrolls away once the camera begins to follow the ship.

To make this an actual GUI, you'll need to create a special GUI layer and stop that layer from scrolling.

1. Return to the Scene Editor and navigate to the Layers Tab.
2. Add a new layer and name it "GUI." **Drag** this layer above the Background layer.
3. Expose the contents of the background layer by **Clicking** on the arrow next to its name and find the actor named "TextLabel."
4. **Drag** only this actor into the new GUI layer and uncheck the "scrollable" box associated with the GUI layer (see Figure 15.7).

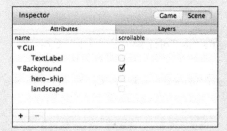

FIGURE 15.7
The TextLabel actor placed on a non-scrolling GUI layer.

5. Save this project for use in the next exercise.

Preview the scene and the TextLabel will remain stationary as the rest of the screen scrolls. You have just made your first non-scrolling GUI!

Tip: The Camera Live Area and Your GUI
When building a GUI on a non-scrolling layer, take special care to build it within the default camera live area (see Figure 15.8), which is indicated by the white outline of the stage. Once a layer is made non-scrollable, only the elements that are placed in this area will display on-screen.

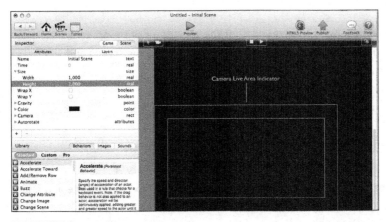

FIGURE 15.8
Non-scrolling GUI's MUST be created withing the camera's live area.

Text Display Box

You can easily create a box to display the text label by changing the Color settings of the actor.

1. Open the TextLabel actor editor. Choose a dark blue color from the color picker and change the Alpha Value to **.25**.

When you **Preview** the scene, the text will now be displayed in a colored box. If the text displayed does not fit within box, the text size and placement can be edited from within the display text behavior.

From a display text behavior you can adjust the alignment of the text (flush left, centered, flush right), the position x and y offset of the text, and the font, size and color of the text (see Figure 15.9).

FIGURE 15.9
The various settings available from a Display Text Behaivor.

GUI Buttons

There are many uses for buttons in a game; at the very least, you'll likely need a "play" and "pause" button. Buttons are created using a combination of Rules and Behaviors.

Exercise 22

Pause Button

In this exercise, you'll create a button to pause the game.

1. Starting with the project from the previous exercise, navigate to the Scenes Editor and create a new scene named "Pause."
2. Go to the Initial Scene and Delete the TextLabel actor from the stage.
3. From the assets folder for Chapter 15, import the image named "Pause.png" to the project.
4. Create a new Actor using this image and open its Editor.
5. Add a Rule to this Actor and create a condition that reads:
    Actor receives event » touch » is » released
6. Nest a Pause Game Behavior in this rule and choose "**Pause**" from the Go to Scene Menu. If you happen to be a pro-user, you will also have the option to display an advertisement. You can ignore this option.
7. Place the Pause Button on the Stage and make sure it is on the GUI layer in the Layers Palette.

Preview the scene and move the space ship around. While you are moving the ship, **Press** the Pause Button and the game will pause. Once paused, the game will seem to be "locked up," but remember, a game (or any computer program) can't do anything it isn't programmed to do. You have not told the game how to return to action yet. To "un-lock" the game you can either click the back button located in the upper left corner of the screen or click the re-play button located directly under the preview button.

***

Tip: The Pause Behavior

Gamesalad's pause behavior pauses the current running scene and displays a new scene on top of it. To display additional information, like the words "Game Paused," add any additional content to the pause scene and it will be displayed on-screen while the game is paused.

***

Button States

Part of good GUI design is to offer the player feedback on their actions. One way of doing this is to give buttons "states" of appearance so they look different depending on the actions of the player. A button's state is often referred to as Normal (the standard appearance of a button), Hover (the appearance of a button when it is being touched by a pointer or finger), and Active (the appearance of a button while it is active).

Exercise 23

Hover State

In this exercise, you'll create a Hover State for the pause button:

1. Return to the Stage and open the pause button's Editor.
2. Add another Rule to the button and set its condition up to read:
   Actor receives event » touch » is » inside
3. Nest a Change Attribute Behavior in the Rule and set it up to read:
   Change Attribute: » self.Color.Alpha » To: » .25
4. Place a copy of this Change Attribute Behavior in the Otherwise section of the Rule and update it to read:
   Change Attribute: » self.Color.Alpha » To: » 1
5. Save this project. You will use it again in another exercise.

Preview the scene and press and hold the mouse button OUTSIDE of the pause button. As you move the mouse pointer in and out of the pause button area, it will highlight as it changes states. Remember, if you accidently click the pause button, the game will seem to "lock-up".

Display Meters

A display meter is an on-screen representation of how much of something the player or another character has in a game. Meters are often used to display a player's health, amount of ammunition available, or the amount of time left in the game. Meters usually display as a solid colored line or a series of images. In the exercises that follow, you'll learn how to create both types.

Exercise 24

Image Display Meter

In this exercise, you will create a life meter that displays a heart image for each life the player has remaining.

1. Open the project from the previous exercise.

2. Open the TextLabel Actor Editor from the previous exercise and update it to read:
    Text: Health: » Align: flush left » Size: 20 » Color: Black

3. Change the Alpha value of this actor to **0**.

4. Place this actor in the upper left hand corner of the stage.

5. Create a new Game Level Integer Attribute named "lives" and set its starting value to 3.

6. Import the image named "Heart.png" to this project and use it to create a new actor. The image is located in the asset files for Chapter 15 folder.

7. Place a copy of the Heart Actor on stage near the TextLabel actor.

8. Open the Heart Actor Editor and add a Replicate Behavior to its list of behaviors. Set up this behavior to read:
    Copies: game.lives » Spacing: 35 (see Figure 15.10)

FIGURE 15.10
The settings of the Replicate Behavior.

Preview the scene and you will see something like Figure 15.11. The scene now displays the word "Health" followed by a series of three hearts. If you're not happy with the exact placement of the actors in the scene, return to the editor and adjust their locations. While this display is nice, it doesn't offer much feedback to the player since there is no interactivity. In the next section, you will update this so the number of hearts decreases when the player loses a life.

FIGURE 15.11
The GUI-heart health meter.

To take a life away from the player, you will set up the player to act like a button—when you click it, the player will lose a life. Of course this would never happen in an actual game. This action is just for demonstration purposes to give you a quick way to take a life away from the player.

1. Open the hero-ship actor's editor and add a Rule. Create a condition that reads:
    Actor receives event » touch » is » pressed
2. Nest a Change Attribute Behavior in the rule and set it up like so:
    Change Attribute: game.lives » to » game.lives-1

Preview the game. Now, when you click the hero-ship, the life count will reduce by one. The number of hearts displayed in the GUI reduces by one as well.

In addition to the image display meter, many games use a solid bar to represent how much of something is remaining in the game. The process for building that sort of GUI meter is very similar to the image display meter.

Exercise 25

Bar Display Meter

In this exercise, you will create a solid bar display meter.

1. Starting with the project you finished in the last exercise, update the value of the Game Level Attribute "lives" to **100**.
2. Delete the Heart actor from the stage.
3. Create a new empty Actor named "HealthBar" and open its Editor.
4. Update the Color of this actor to green, or any other color you like.
5. Change this actor's Width to **1** and Height to **20**.
6. Add a Replicate Behavior to this actor and set it up to read:
   Copies: game.lives » Spacing: 1
7. Add this Actor to the Stage, on the right hand side of the TextLabel actor.

When you **Preview** the scene, you will see a long green bar extending across the top of the screen (see Figure 15.12). Clicking on the player's ship will reduce the lives value. As you click the ship, the bar will shrink.

FIGURE 15.12
The GUI-bar health meter.

Tip: Creating the Bar

The "bar" in the pervious exercise is created by repeating a one pixel wide line over and over, one hundred times. When the player loses a life, one pixel of the line is removed, causing the bar to decrease in length.

Summary

In this chapter, you learned about the camera's controls and settings. You learned how to use the Control Camera Behavior to create a camera that will follow an actor as the actor moves throughout the scene. Next, you learned how to create a non-scrolling GUI layer. Finally, you learned how to create some common GUI elements and experimented with creating many of them yourself.

Chapter 16
Game 3 – Box Breaker

In This Chapter You Will Learn:

» How to design the game Box Breaker

» How to build the actors for Box Breaker

» How to create the scenes/levels for Box Breaker

» How to build a GUI for Box Breaker

» How to add sounds to Box Breaker

In this chapter, you will make a physics puzzle game called Box Breaker. You will begin the chapter by establishing the game's concept, rules, and requirements. You will then create all of the actors needed for the game and build one full level of the game. Then you will add a GUI to the scene and include sounds in the game. Finally, you will make copies of the completed scene and create additional levels for the game.

Note: Completed Project File
A completed version of the project for this chapter is available for reference in the Assets Folder for Chapter 16.

Game Concept

The concept of Box Breaker, a physics puzzle game, is to remove all of the breakable boxes from the play area either by clicking on them with the mouse pointer or by pushing them beyond the screen bounds. Each scene of the game will be a different puzzle that needs to be solved in order to move to the next scene.

Game Rules

The rules of Box Breaker are:

» Each level will have a certain number of boxes that must be broken or removed before the player can move to the next level.

» Some boxes in the game are unbreakable.

» There will be a "special" box type that will reset the level if it is removed from the screen.

» Boxes can be broken by clicking on them or removed from the level by moving them beyond the scene's bounds.

Game Requirements

Box Breaker will require many actors, images, and sounds. A starter file named "Box Breaker-Starter" is located in the assets folder for chapter 16. The requirements for the game are:

» The game will be built to play in the Gamesalad Arcade.

» The game will use physics to control the interactions of the boxes.

You will need:

» Three game attributes: one for the total number of boxes per level, one to indicate the game level number, and one to indicate the win/loss state of the game.

» Sixteen different actors that include five box type actors and four GUI actors.

» A game controller.

» A trigger actor to detect if any boxes leave the play area.

» Sound effects.

Game Setup

To start the project, open the file named "Box Breaker-Starter" located in the assets folder for chapter 16. Take a moment to look through the project and note that is has been set up to use the Gamesalad Arcade Platform. There is one scene, nine images, and two sounds provided in the file and a value of 400 has been applied to the gravity y setting in the scene attributes tab.

Game Attributes

Since some of the actors that will be created later in the game will need to reference the three game level attributes, you should create those first. In the Inspector Palette, open the Attributes Tab and add two Integer Attributes and one Boolean Attribute to the list. Set them up like so:

1.   Name the first Integer Attribute "total" and give it a starting value of **0**. This attribute will be used on each scene to keep track of the total number of boxes that need to be removed from the level to win.

2. Name the second Integer Attribute "level." Its starting value should be **1**. This attribute will keep track of what level the player is on.

3. Finally, name the Boolean Attribute "winnable" and give it a starting value of **true** (check the check box). This attribute will keep track of whether or not the game is winnable. The game will not be winnable if the "special" box is removed from the level.

Game Actors

To create the actual play area for the game, **Drag** the first four images ("background," "wood-cracked," "wood-solid," and "wood-plank") to the Actors Tab to create four Actors.

Tip: Zero Physics

Several of the actors in Box Breaker will have their physics settings "zeroed out." Turning off the actors' physics settings like this can help reduce any lag Gamesalad might experience during a complex physics-based game. You should only zero out these settings for actors that will never be affected by physics in the game, like a background image.

---

1. Open the background Actor Editor and change these settings in the Physics Settings:
    Density 0 » Friction 0 » Bounciness 0 » Movable Off

2. Add this Actor to the Scene and update its X and Y position so it's positioned at the exact center of the scene (240,160).

3. Next, open the editor for the wood-cracked actor and update these settings:
    Graphics: **Horizontal Wrap Tile » Vertical Wrap Tile**
    Physics: **Density 5 » Friction 15 » Bounciness 0.1 » Drag 15**

Note: Physics

The numbers used in the physics settings for this game were determined through trial and error so the objects work as needed in order to solve the puzzles that will be built. Feel free to adjust the numbers once you have completed the project to see how different settings affect the game play.

---

4. Apply these same Graphics and Physics settings to the wood-solid Actor.

5. For the wood-plank Actor, apply the same setting, but also turn movable **off** within the Physics Settings.

6. Next, create an Actor from the "glass" image and set its Physics Settings like so:
    Density 5 » Friction 10 » Bounciness 0.1

7. Finally, use the "stone" image to create an Actor and update these settings:
    Graphics: **Horizontal Wrap Tile » Vertical Wrap Tile**
    Physics: **Density 10 » Friction 20 » Bounciness 0.1 » Movable Off**

With all of the box actors added to the game, the next step is to set up the basic collision actions for each actor so the first level of the game can be created.

1. Navigate to the Actors Tab from the Home Screen.
2. Add a new Tag named "Solid" to the tags column.
3. **Drag** the five box actors (not the background) into the "Solid" tag.
4. **Double-Click** the wood-cracked actor and add a Collide Behavior to it. Set it up to read:
    Bounce when colliding with: » actor with tag » Solid
5. **Copy** this behavior and **Paste** it in the "wood-solid" and "glass" Actors.

Note: Actor Editor

You are able to open an actor's editor by double-clicking the actor within the Actors Tab as well as in the Stage Editor.

---

6. Return to the Stage Editor for Level 1 and use the actors you just created to build a scene that looks like Figure 16.1.

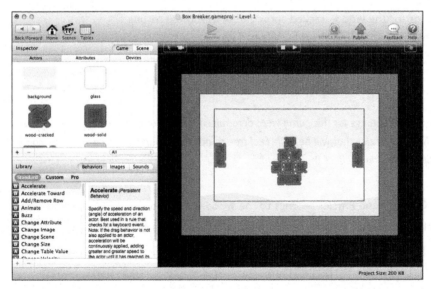

FIGURE 16.1
The Level 1 Scene with 6 wood-cracked actors and 3 wood-plank actors placed on Stage.

When your scene matches the figure above, press **Preview** and you will see that all of the boxes just sit on-screen—trying to click or move them will have no effect yet. In the following steps, you'll add interactivity to the game, but first you'll need to add a couple more actors:

1. First, use the "pop" image to create a new Actor. Open its Actor Editor and zero out its Physics Settings like you did for the background Actor, making sure to Uncheck Movable. Also change its Height and Width to **16**.

2. Next, add an empty actor, by **Clicking** the **Plus (+)** button in the Actors Tab. Name this actor "trigger." Zero out its Physics Settings and Uncheck Movable.

3. Place three copies of the trigger Actor around the left, right, and bottom edges of the stage (see Figure 16.2). The "trigger" actor will act as exactly that, a trigger that will tell the game when any boxes have fallen beyond of the scene's bounds.

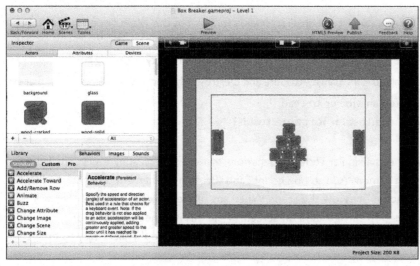

FIGURE 16.2
Copies of the Trigger Actor have been placed and the left, right and bottom edges of the Stage pasteboard.

4. Open the wood-cracked Actor Editor and add a Rule. Name it "Break me when I'm touched." Set this rule's condition up to read:
   Actor receives event » touch » is » pressed

5. Nest three Behaviors in this rule: a Spawn Actor, Change Attribute, and a Destroy Behavior in that order, from top to bottom.

6. Set the Spawn Actor Behavior up to read:
   Actor: pop

7. Configure the Change Attribute to read:

   Change Attribute: game.total » To: game.total-1

8. Outside of this rule, add another Change Attribute behavior. Name it "Add to box count" and set it up to read:

   Change Attribute: game.total » To: game.total+1

Tip: Instant Action

Placing an action behavior [A], like change attribute, outside of a rule in an actor causes that behavior to immediately perform its action when the actor is placed on the stage during the game. So, the change attribute behavior in the wood-cracked actor will immediately fire when the actor appears on-screen. It will increase the total number of boxes, the "total" game attribute, by 1.

---

9. Finally, add another Rule to the list of behaviors. Name it "Destroy me when I'm off screen" and create one condition that reads:

   Actor receives event » overlaps or collides » with » actor of type » trigger

10. Nest two Behaviors in this rule: a Change Attribute and Destroy Behavior (list the behaviors in that order).

11. Set the Change Attribute behavior up to read:

    Change Attribute: game.total » To: game.total-1

The wood-plank actor will need a similar series of behaviors. Instead of recreating everything from scratch, **Copy** the behaviors named "Add to box count" and "Break me when I'm touched" and **Paste** them into the wood-plank actor. **Preview** the scene. When any of the boxes are clicked, they will disappear. Unfortunately, the "pop" image stays on-screen. While this isn't necessarily wrong, it would look a lot nicer if the "pop" image was animated—it would seem more like a pop! That is easy to fix.

1. Open the pop Actor Editor and add a Play Sound Behavior. Choose the sound "pop" from the drop-down menu.

2. Add an Interpolate Behavior and set it up to read:

   Interpolate Attribute: self.Size.Width » To: 32 » Duration: .1

3. Make a copy of the Interpolate Behavior and set the copy up to read:

   Interpolate Attribute: self.Size.Height » To: 32 » Duration: .1

4. For the sake of organization, nest those two interpolate behaviors in a group and name the group "Grow the pop image."

5. Add another Interpolate Behavior and set it up to read:

   Interpolate Attribute: self.Rotation » To: 90 » Duration: 2

6. Add a Timer to the list and set it to read:

    After .15 seconds » Check Run to Completion

7. Finally, nest a Destroy Behavior in the Timer.

Tip: Forced Rotation

Since the pop actor was created as a non-movable actor in its physics settings, a standard Rotate Behavior will have no effect on it. To rotate the "pop," it must be "forced" by using an Interpolate Behavior. Interpolate Behaviors work outside of the physics engine, allowing movement to be forced when it otherwise would not be allowed by the engine.

The game is progressing nicely; you should be able to clear the screen of boxes by clicking them or dropping them out of the screen and the pop effect should now animate and make a popping sound! Preview the game and check it out.

The final box to finish is the "wood-solid" actor. To make this update as quick and easy as possible, start by opening the editor for the "wood-cracked" actor and **Copy** the behaviors named "Add to box count" and "Destroy me when I'm off screen." **Paste** copies of these two behaviors into the "wood-solid" actor. After adding those two behaviors, there is just one additional rule to add:

1. Add a Rule to the actor and name it "Play sound if I'm touched." Create a condition that reads:

    Actor receives event » touch » is » pressed

2. Nest a Play Sound Behavior in the Rule and choose the sound "clunk" from the drop-down menu.

The next big step in the game is to add some feedback for the player.

Game GUI

The GUI for Box Breaker will contain four elements:

1. Some on-screen text displaying the number of boxes left to be removed from the game.
2. An on-screen text displaying what level is currently being played.
3. A pause button.
4. A level reset button. It will be possible for the player to create an unwinnable situation in the game, so for this reason, the player will need a way to reset the level and try again.

Begin by creating a GUI layer in the layers tab of the scene palette. There is no need to make the layer non-scrollable, but it's always helpful to keep all of the GUI elements isolated so they are easy to access during development. Once the GUI layer has been added, create the text display actors:

1. Add a new empty Actor to the project and name it "box display." Set the Alpha Value of the Actor to **0**. Zero out the Physics Settings and Uncheck Moveable.

Note: Moveable and Gravity

Every actor placed on the stage will be affected by the gravity that was applied earlier in this exercise. To stop the GUI elements from dropping off the scene, it is important to make them all non-moveable.

---

2. Add a Display Text Behavior and name it "GUI display for boxes." Use the Text Expression Editor to create an expression that reads:
    "Boxes\32Remaining:\32"..game.total
3. Set up the Font options as:
    Align: Left » Font: Helvetica Neue » Size: 20 » Color Blue
4. Return to the Actors Tab in the Inspector Palette and make a copy of the "box display" actor. Rename this copy "level display."
5. Change the level display Actor's Text Expression of the Display Text Behavior to read:
    "Level:\32"..game.level
6. Finally, update the level display Actor's Alignment to:
    Align: Right

Note: Expression vs. Text Input

When typing a complex expression into the expression editor box, you MUST use the "e" button to open the expression editor. Simply typing the expression into the text input box will not work as expected.

---

7. Return to the Stage and place the two new actors on-screen. Place the box display Actor at a Position of (56,300) and the level display Actor at a Position of (420,300).
8. To create the buttons for the GUI, create two Actors using the images named "button-pause" and "button-reload".
9. Open the button-reload Actor Editor. Zero out its Physics, Uncheck Moveable, and set its Alpha Value to **0.5**.

10. Add a Rule to the Actor and name it "Reset the level." Create one condition to read:
    Actor receives event » touch » is » pressed

11. Nest two Change Attribute Behaviors and a Reset Scene Behavior in the rule.

12. Make the first Change Attribute read:
    Change Attribute: game.total » To: 0

13. Make the second Change Attribute read:
    Change Attribute: game.winnable » To: true

14. Place this button on stage at the position (24,24).

Tip: Resetting a Scene

When resetting a scene in a game, you might think that is a simple as adding a reset scene behavior. While this behavior does reset the actual scene, it DOES NOT reset any game level attributes that are used in that scene. If any game level attributes need to be reset, that will need to be done manually during the scene reset using change attribute behaviors.

Before the pause button will correctly work, a new pause scene will have to be added to the game. Navigate to the Scenes Tab and add a new Scene named "Paused" to the project. Open the new scene to view its Stage:

1. Add a new empty Actor to the growing list of actors and name this one "Game Paused." Open the Actor Editor, zero out its Physics, and Uncheck Movable.

2. Under the Color settings for the Actor, choose **Black** from the color picker and change the Alpha Value to **0.75**.

3. Add a Display Text Behavior to this Actor and set it up like so:
   Text: Game Paused » Size: 50

4. Add a Rule and create a condition that reads:
   Actor receives event » touch » is » pressed

5. Nest an Unpause Game Behavior in the rule.

6. Return to the Stage, for the Paused scene, and place this Actor at a Position of (240,160).

7. **Drag** the edges of the Actor so it extends to the left and right edge of the Stage (see Figure 16.3).

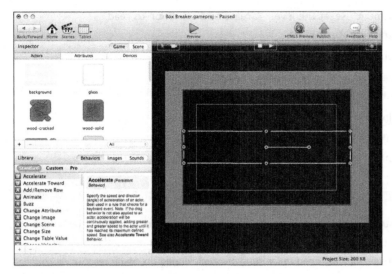

FIGURE 16.3
The "Game-Paused" actor added to the "Paused" Scene.

Now that the actual pause scene is built, the pause button can be created. Return to the Stage Editor for the Scene named "Level 1" and open the Editor for the Actor named "button-pause."

1. Zero out the Physics Settings for the pause button, Uncheck Moveable, and change its Alpha Value to **0.5**.
2. Add a Rule and create a condition that reads:
   Actor receives event » touch » is » pressed
3. Nest a Pause Game Behavior in the Rule and choose the Paused Scene from the drop-down Go To Scene menu.
4. Finally, place this button on the Stage at a Position of (454,24).
5. Return to the Layers Tab and make sure the four GUI elements are on the correct layer. If some actors are placed on the wrong layer, **Drag** them into the GUI layer.

Preview the game and you will see a fully working GUI, displaying the correct information and a fully working game (see Figure 16.4).

You could just about call this a complete level at this point; however, there are a couple small points that should be addressed. Once all of the boxes have been removed from the level, the game should display a message of success or failure to the player and move to the next level if the level was completed correctly. A game controller will be needed to make that happen.

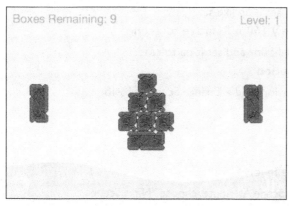

FIGURE 16.4
The completed scene with the fully functional GUI.

Game Controller

One of the actions of the game control actor is to display messages of success or failure to the player. Each message will be a separate actor that displays the appropriate text message to the player.

1. To create the first message, add a new empty Actor in the Actors Palette and name it "Level Up!"
2. Zero this actor's Physics Settings, Uncheck Movable, and change its Alpha Value to **0**.
3. Next, add a Display Text Behavior and enter the following text into the text field: "Level Up!"
4. Close this Actor's Editor and make a copy of this actor. Name the copy "Replay Level."
5. Open the new Actor's Editor and change the text in the Display Text Behavior to read: "Replay the Level…"

After the two messages have been created, you can create the game controller and finish off a complete level of the game by:

1. Create a new empty Actor and name it "controller." Zero this actor's Physics and Uncheck Moveable.
2. Add a Rule and name it "Run this when the level is complete." Create the rule's condition to read:
    Attribute » game.total » equals (=) » 0.0
3. Nest a Timer Behavior in the rule and set it up to read:
    After » 1 » seconds » Check Run to Completion
4. Nest a Rule inside this Timer and set its condition to read:
    Attribute » game.winnable » is » true

5. Nest a Spawn Actor Behavior inside the Rule and set it up like so:
    Actor: Level Up! » Position x 240 » Position y 160 » Relative to: scene

6. Nest a Timer Behavior below the Spawn Actor Behavior and set it up to read:
    After » 1 » seconds » check Run to Completion

7. Inside this Timer, nest two Change Attribute Behaviors and a Change Scene Behavior.

8. Set up the first Change Attribute to read:
    Change Attribute » game.total » To: » 0

9. Set the second Change Attribute to read:
    Change Attribute » game.level » to » game.level+1

10. Finally, from the drop-down menu of the Change Scene Attribute, choose "Next Scene."

The completed rule should look like Figure 16.5:

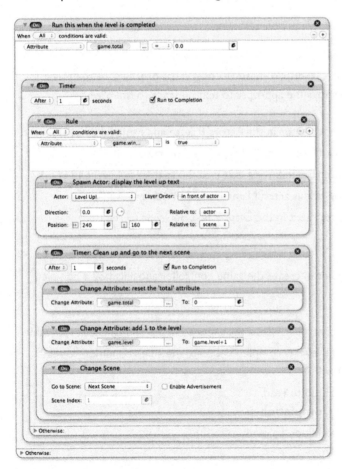

FIGURE 16.5
The completed "Run this when the level is completed" rule.

Note: What's going on in the "Run this when the level is complete" rule?

The rule you just created is by far the most complex rule you have created yet, take a moment to examine exactly how it performs. The first thing it does is check and make sure all of the boxes have been removed from the scene (game.total = 0). If they have, the game will wait one second to allow all of the objects to fall out of the screen's bounds. If, after that second passes, the game is still "winnable" (game.winnable = true), the winning message will be shown on-screen. One second after the message is displayed, the game will load the next level.

To complete the game controller, you will add a rule to handle the losing conditions:

1. Add another Rule to the controller and name it "Run this when the level is failed." Set this rule's condition to read:
    Attribute » game.winnable » is » false
2. Nest a Spawn Actor Behavior in the Rule and make it read:
    Actor: Replay Level » Position x 240 » Position y 160 » Relative to: scene
3. Nest a Timer Behavior in this same Rule and set it up to read:
    After » 1 » seconds » check Run to Completion
4. Nest two Change Attribute Behaviors and a Reset Scene Behavior in the Timer.
5. Make the first Change Attribute Behavior read:
    Change Attribute » game.winnable » To: » true
6. Set the second Change Attribute up to read:
    Change Attribute » game.total » To: » 0

Now that the game controller actor is created, return to the stage and place a copy of the actor in the pasteboard area of the stage.

Before playtesting the game, there is one final addition that must be made to the glass actor. If this actor falls out of the screen, it should update the winnable attribute to false so the game is no longer winnable.

1. Open the glass Actor's Editor and add a Rule. Create a condition in the Rule to read:
    Actor receives event » overlaps ore collides » with » actor of type » trigger
2. Nest a Change Attribute Behavior in the rule and make it read:
    Change Attribute: game.winnable » To: » false

Preview the game. Once you have cleared all of the boxes, the game will load the next scene.

Note: Bug Squashing

Remember, if you have any problems or end up with any errors in the behaviors, there is a fully working version of this game in the assets folder for chapter 16. You can use that finished file for reference to help you troubleshoot any bugs.

As you probably noticed, once you finished the level, the game loads the pause scene instead of a new level to play. To make this a more complete gaming experience, you should build more levels using the actors you have created. Below are a few screen shots of the finished levels you'll find in the completed version of the game that is provided for reference (see Figure 16.5). You can also use your imagination and create something totally new and different!

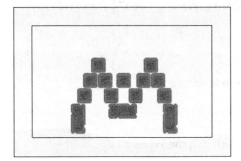

FIGURE 16.5A
Level 2 of the completed game.

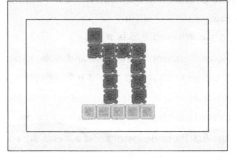

FIGURE 16.5B
Level 3 of the completed game.

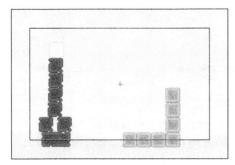

FIGURE 16.5C
Level 4 of the completed game.

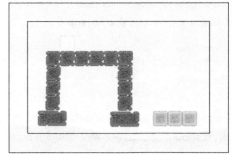

FIGURE 16.5D
Level 5 of the completed game.

Summary

In the last chapter, you created a fully functional physics puzzle game. You started by figuring out what the game's rules and assets would be. Then you constructed the first level of the game, adding all of the necessary actors and behaviors. Next, you added a GUI display that featured buttons and text displays for the player's reference. Finally, you added a game controller to handle the win and loss conditions of the game.

Chapter 17
Animation and Particles

In This Chapter You Will Learn:

» What animation is

» How to use the animate behavior

» How to create frames of animation

» How to animate static images using behaviors

» How to create particle effects

You will begin this chapter by learning about animation, how to create frames of animation, and how to use the animate behavior. Next, you will learn how to use some of Gamesalad's motion related behaviors to create animations using static sprites. Afterwards, you will learn about the particles behavior and how to use it to create special effects for your games. Finally, you'll create a particle emitter.

Animation

Gamesalad uses frame-based animation, also known as traditional cel animation, to animate sprites. Frame-based animation is an animation technique where each frame is individually created, either by hand or on a computer. Each frame of an animation slightly differs from the previous frame. When the frames are played in succession, the sprite will appear to move on-screen.

The Animate Behavior

The Animate Behavior is used to incorporate frame-based animations in Gamesalad games (see Figure 17.1). The Animate Behavior provides several options for adjusting an animation:

FIGURE 17.1
Gamesalads Animate Behavior.

» **Frames:** Drag images, which will be used as the frames of the animation, from the images tab.

» **Speed:** The number of frames per second (fps) at which the animation will run. The larger the number, the faster the animation will run.

» **Loop:** Checking this box will cause the animation to replay once it reaches its final frame.

» **Restore:** Checking this box will show the image used for the actor once the animation stops playing. This will only have an effect if "Loop" is not checked.

Exercise 26

Animate a Walking Sprite

In this exercise, you will create a sprite that walks on the stage using individual frames of animation.

1. Open the file named "walk-animation" from the Asset Folder for Chapter 17. This file contains eight frames of animation already imported into the Images Tab.

2. Create an Actor using the image named "walk-01."

3. Open the Actor Editor and add an Animate Behavior to it.

4. Drag the eight images (in numeric order) into the Animate Behavior, starting with walk-01.

5. Return to the Scene Editor and place the Actor on the Stage.

6. **Preview** the Scene and watch the little guy walk in place!

7. Save this exercise. You'll use it again in this chapter.

Note: Lots of Images

If the animation you are creating contains a lot of individual frames, the frames can be named in sequential order by adding a trailing number. You can then select all the images at one time and drop them into an Animate Behavior and the images will be added in the order they are numbered.

Animation Frames

When you, or your artist, create frames of animation for use in Gamesalad, keep in mind that every individual frame of an animation **must** have the same pixel dimensions. The largest frame size will dictate the size of every other frame of animation. For example:

Every image in the walk cycle animation used in the previous example is 79 pixels wide and 146 pixels high. The height is determined by frame 4 of the walk cycle and the width is determined by frame 6. Not every frame fills that width and height. For example, frame 7 has a lot of "dead space" on its right and left edges.

While it may be tempting to crop any "dead space" out of the frames, don't do it! Gamesalad creates the main actor that the animation runs within at a specific pixel size. If the frames of animation used don't exactly match this size, they will automatically be resized while the animation plays to fit the overall pixel dimensions and the animation will warp and resize as it's played.

Exercise 27

Warping Animation

In this exercise, as a demonstration of what not to do, you'll create an animation using frames with different pixel dimensions.

1. Open the previous exercise and import the "cropped" image frames. These are located in the Assets Folder for Chapter 17.

2. Open the current Actor and delete the frames of animation, leaving the actual Animate Behavior.

3. In numeric order, add the "cropped" frames to the Animate Behavior. You may need to increase the size of the preview image to read the entire file name.

4. **Preview** the scene. This time, you'll notice that the animation is not quite right. The most noticeable change is the head of the character pulsates, but also the line weights change from frame to frame. Return to the Animate Behavior and slow the speed to 1 fps—you will be able to clearly see how each frame is stretched to fit the actor's overall pixel dimensions at this slow speed.

5. Don't bother to save this mess, but still keep the previous version for the next exercise.

Note: Manipulating Frames

Individual frames of the animation can be selected, moved, and deleted from within the Animate Behavior. To delete a frame, click on it and press the Delete Key. To reorder frames, select a frame and drag it within the Animate Behavior. As it is moved, a blue line will indicate its placement. Release the mouse button and the frame will be placed at this new location.

Depending on the animation, its size, and content, the effects of this warping could be more or less pronounced. However, you can avoid them all together by creating all of the animation's frames at the same pixel dimensions.

Behavior Animations

Frame-based animation isn't the only way sprites can be animated in Gamesalad. As you've already seen in previous lessons, there are a lot of Behaviors available to move actors around the stage. Some of these behaviors include:

» Accelerate

» Accelerate Toward

» Change Size

» Interpolate

» Move

» Move To

» Rotate

» Rotate to Angle

» Rotate to Position

All of those behaviors can be used to animate sprites within Gamesalad to create simple or complex animations.

Exercise 28

Walk the Character Across the Stage

In this exercise, you'll add a Move Behavior to the actor from the previous exercise to make it "walk" across the stage.

1. Open your file from the first exercise in this chapter.
2. Open the Actore Editor for the walk-01 actor and add a Move Behavior below the Animate Behavior.
3. Set up the Move Behavior to read:
    Relative to: scene » Speed: 40
4. Make sure the Speed setting in the Animate Behavior is 10 fps.
5. Return to the Stage and **Drag** the actor to the gray Pasteboard on the left side of the Stage.
6. When you **Preview** the scene, the actor will trot across the screen.

By combining a frame-based animation with a Behavior, you are able to create an animated character that is very reminiscent of a cartoon you may see on television.

Behaviors can be used to create many kinds of animations. For example, an Accelerate Behavior can be combined with a Rotate Behavior to drop and rotate snowflakes from the top of the stage in a Christmas themed game. While the game's title screen is displayed, the name of the game could be faded in and out using Interpolate Behaviors. For a platform game, a bridge can be created that periodically rotates (using a Rotate Behavior) to a new angle and location. The possibilities are truly only limited by your own imagination!

Exercise 29

Snow

In this exercise, you'll take one of the ideas mentioned above and bring it to life—snow.

1. Open the file named "snow" from the Asset Files Folder for Hour 17. This file already has two actors created and one placed on stage. You'll add all the behaviors needed to make everything work.

2. In this case, you will use the background sky actor as the game controller. Open the Actor Editor for the "sky" actor.

3. Add a Timer Behavior and set it up to read:
    Every » 0.1 » seconds » check Run to Completion

4. Nest a Spawn Actor Behavior in the Timer and set it to read:
    Actor: » snow-flake » Position x » random(0,568) » Position y » 370 » Relative to: scene

5. Open the Actore Editor for the snowflake actor and add an Accelerate and Rotate Behavior.

6. Set the Accelerate Behavior to read:
    Direction 270 » Acceleration 100 » Relative to: scene

7. Make the Rotate Behavior read:
    Direction: Clockwise » Speed: random(50,200)

8. **Preview** the scene and watch the snow fall!

Tip: Accelerate Relative to Scene

In the previous exercise, the Accelerate Behavior in the snowflake actor was created to accelerate relative to the scene. In this case, that is a very important step since the actor is also rotating as it moves on the stage. If the acceleration were relative to the actor instead, the snowflakes would not move in a predictable way because the direction of acceleration would change as the actor rotates.

Particles

A particle is a sprite that is emitted, or added to the scene, by an actor with a Particles Behavior applied to it. These particles can be almost anything you can imagine. They can be large or small, move quickly or slowly, they can be colorful or translucent. Particles can be used to create all kinds of special effects and animations in a game; you can create realistic fire and smoke effects, create rain and weather effects, or even create an endless star field. Anytime particles are added to a game to create an effect, it is commonly called a particle effect.

Particles Behavior

The Particles Behavior is probably one of the most complex looking behaviors Gamesalad has to offer. It consists of a series of six tabs, each with their own set of controls that are used to dictate everything from an individual particle's color, to its speed of movement and rotation on-screen. If you take the time to master the Particles Behavior, you will be rewarded with the ability to create all kinds of otherwise impossible special effects.

Note: Particle Collisions
While each particle is a sprite just like any actor in Gamesalad, particles do not collide with each other or with other actors in the game—they act as scenery objects only.

Spawn Rate Tab

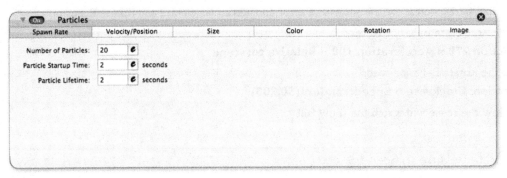

FIGURE 17.2
The Spawn Rate tab of the Particle Behavior.

» **Number of Particles:** This literally is the number of particles that the behavior will attempt to spawn. I say attempt because depending on the startup time and particle lifetime value below, all of the particles may not be spawned. A timer behavior can also influence the number of particles spawned if the particle behavior is contained within one. The higher this number, the larger the number of particles spawned. If a very high number of particles are required, sometimes it is more effective to use multiple particle behaviors with a lower "Number of Particles" setting. For example, if 600 particles are required for an effect, it may make sense to use three particle Behaviors set to spawn 200 particles each. This can only be determined through trial and error while creating the effect.

» **Particle Startup Time:** This controls how quickly the particles begin to spawn once their trigger event occurs. If a low number like .5 is used, Gamesalad will quickly spawn all of the particles to the screen. If particles should spawn more slowly over time, a higher number like 5 or 10 should be used in this input box. Low numbers will cause a quick burst of particles to be displayed while higher numbers will create a constant stream of particles.

» **Particle Lifetime:** This value is also expressed as seconds and literally is the number of seconds each particle will be visible on-screen (or how long it will live off-screen if it moves past the edge of the screen). Once this time limit has passed, Gamesalad will respawn more particles in an attempt to keep the "Number of Particles" consistent on-screen.

Tip: Timers and Particles

Since the particle behavior will continually spawn particles, the behavior is often combined with a timer behavior to help control the timing of the particles. For example, to create a particle-based explosion that will be displayed one time only, the particle behavior should be enclosed in a "For" timer behavior that allows the particles to only spawn once for a very short time. You'll see an example of this in the game "Geometry Runner" that you will create in chapter 20.

Velocity/Position Tab

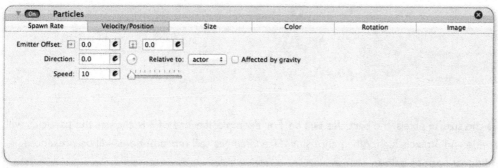

FIGURE 17.3
The Velocity/Position tab of the Particle Behavior.

» **Emitter Offset:** Like all actors in Gamesalad, the actor that is used to spawn the particle's origin point is the center point of that actor. When the emitter offset value is set to 0, particles will be spawned from the center point of this actor. To change the point particles are spawned from, enter some other value in the horizontal (arrow pointing right) and vertical (arrow pointing up) offset input boxes.

» **Direction:** This is the direction the particles will move once they are spawned on stage. This can be relative to the actor or the scene. Particles can also be affected by gravity in the scene. For particles to be affected by gravity, a value **must** be entered for the X and/or Y gravity value in the scene palette.

» **Speed:** This indicates how quickly the particles will move in their chosen direction. The higher the number, the faster they will move.

Tip: Randomness

The particle behavior is a great place to use the expression editor combined with the random function for many of the particles settings. The particles will feel much more natural when randomness is introduced. For example, if particles were being used to create a snowstorm effect, each flake of snow would likely be a different size, move at a slightly different speed, and even have subtle color variations from every other flake. All of that variation can be accomplished using the random function.

Size Tab

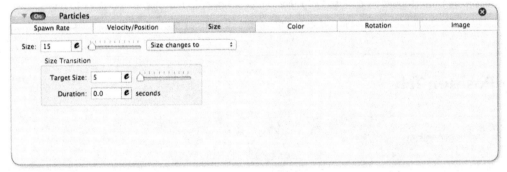

FIGURE 17.4
The Size tab of the Particle Behavior.

» **Size:** This is the size, in pixels, the particles will be. For example, if a size of 3 is chosen, the particles will be 3 pixels wide and 3 pixels high. When choosing "Size Changes to," more options will be presented with the additional options below.

» **Target Size:** This is the size, in pixels, the particles will either grow or shrink to. The particles will grow if the original size is lower than the target size and they will shrink if the original size is larger than the target size.

» **Duration:** This is the number of seconds the size transition will take. Note that it's possible to use this size tab to alter the apparent life span of the particles. Imagine particles have been given a particle lifetime of 10 seconds in the spawn rate tab. But in the size tab, they have been set to shrink to a size of 0 with duration of 5 seconds. During game play, the particles would seem to disappear after 5 seconds instead of the expected 10 seconds.

Color Tab

Use the settings of the color tab to color tint or completely change the color of particles, depending on the image used for the particle. When a full color image is used as a particle, choosing a color in the color tab will tint the full color image with the chosen color. When using a gray scale image as a particle, choosing a color in the color tab will completely change the color of the image. The white areas of the image will have full intensity of the chosen color and the gray areas will be less intense.

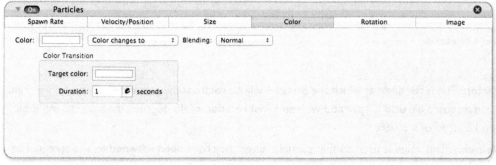

FIGURE 17.5
The Color tab of the Particle Behavior.

» **Color:** Use the standard color picker to colorize or tint the particle image. Using the opacity slider, you can make the color translucent. When used in conjunction with the blending mode drop-down menu, some nice effects can be achieved. When choosing "Color Changes to," two more options will be presented.

» **Target Color:** When a target color is chosen, the particle's color will change over time, transitioning from its starting color to the target color.

» **Duration:** This is the number of seconds it will take for the particle to transition from its starting color to the target color.

Note: Particle Lifetime

It's possible to use the color tab to alter the apparent life span of the particles. For example, let's say the particles have been given a particle lifetime of 10 seconds in the spawn rate tab, but in the color tab, they have been set to transition to a color with a 0% alpha value with a duration of 5 seconds. When playing the game, the particles would seem to disappear after 5 seconds instead of the expected 10.

Rotation Tab

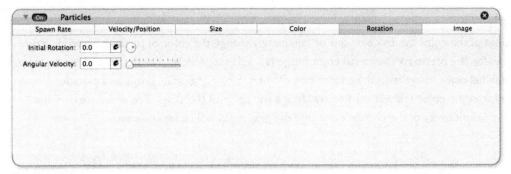

FIGURE 17.6
The Rotation tab of the Particle Behavior.

» **Initial Rotation:** This is the angle at which the particles will be rotated when they are spawned on-screen. For example, if a square particle is spawned with an initial rotation of 45 degrees, the particle will look like a diamond instead of a square.

» **Angular Velocity:** This value is used to spin particles after they have been spawned to the screen. The higher the number, the faster the particles will spin. Positive values will make the particles to spin counter-clockwise and negative values will spin the particles clockwise.

Image Tab

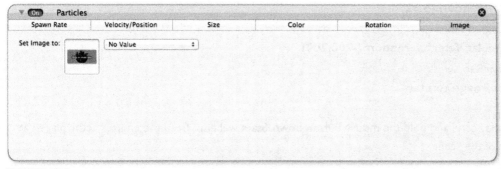

FIGURE 17.7
The Image tab of the Particle Behavior.

» **Set Image To:** Drag an image to the open box or choose an image from the drop-down menu and that image will be used for the particle. Any image that can be imported into Gamesalad can be used as a particle.

Note: No Image
If no image is chosen for the particle, Gamesalad will use a basic square pixel for the particle's image.

Exercise 30

Stars Particles
In this exercise, you'll create an actor that emits stars when the mouse button is clicked.

1. Open the starter file for this exercise named "stars." It is located in the Asset Folder for Chapter 17.
2. Open the Actore Editor for the emitter Actor and add a Rule with a conditions that reads:
   Actor receives event » mouse button » is » down
3. Nest a Particles Behavior in the rule and set the tabs up as indicated below:
   a. Spawn Rate Tab:
      Number of Particles 100 » Particle Startup Time: 4 » Particle Lifetime 4
   b. Velocity/Position Tab:
      Direction: random(0,359) » Relative to scene » Speed: random(50,200)

    c. Size Tab:
       Size: random(5,32)

    d. Rotation Tab:
       Angular Velocity: random(-200,200)

    e. Image Tab:
       Set Image to: star

Preview the scene and hold the mouse button down. Stars will emit from the emitter actor placed at the center of the scene.

Tip: Emitter Actor Transparency

The transparency of the emitter actor is separate from the transparency of the particles, so making the emitter invisible by setting its Alpha Value to 0 will not affect the transparency of the particles emitted.

Summary

In this chapter, you learned all about animation. You started the hour by learning about the animate behavior. Then you learned how to create animations from static images by combining them with Gamesalad's included movement behaviors. Finally, you learned all about the particles behavior, what all the tabs are for, and how to create particle emitters. In the final exercise, you created your own particle emitter.

Chapter 18
Tables

In This Chapter You Will Learn:

» What tables are

» How to create a table

» How to use table related behaviors

» How to use table related functions

In this chapter, you will learn about tables in Gamesalad. You will begin by learning what tables are and what they can be used for. Afterwards, you will learn about the table related behaviors Gamesalad has to offer. Finally, you will learn about table related functions and how to use them to manipulate the data stored in tables.

Table Basics

Tables are collections of data on which all sorts of functions can be performed. Data can be saved, reordered, rewritten, and recalled for use in Gamesalad projects. If you are familiar with spreadsheet software, tables are essentially spreadsheets. There are so many uses for tables that it's impossible to put them into one single category. Throughout this chapter, you'll work on several exercises that will show you some of the many possible uses for tables.

Tables are created from the Tables Tab located in the Home screen. All Gamesalad projects include one default table named "PurchaseTable." This table is used by Gamesalad when performing In App Purchases and cannot be deleted. Tables are created and deleted by using the plus (+) and minus (-) buttons located in the lower left corner of the screen (see Figure 18.1).

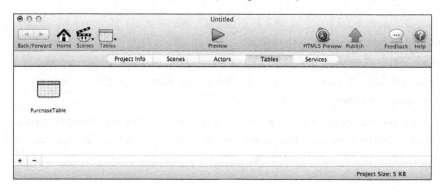

FIGURE 18.1
The Tables Tab.

When a table is created, a new table will be added to the list of available tables; from there, the table can be renamed and opened by double-clicking it. All tables begin with one row and one column of information— from this base, additional rows and columns can be added. See Figure 18.2 for a detailed description of the table editor.

Tip: Table Names

Table names show up in the Expression Editor and Attributes Browser, along with all of the project's attributes. It can be difficult to distinguish a table name from an attribute name so it's a good idea to begin your table names with something significant and recognizable. Consider something like "TABLE" or "DATA" or anything you find easily recognizable.

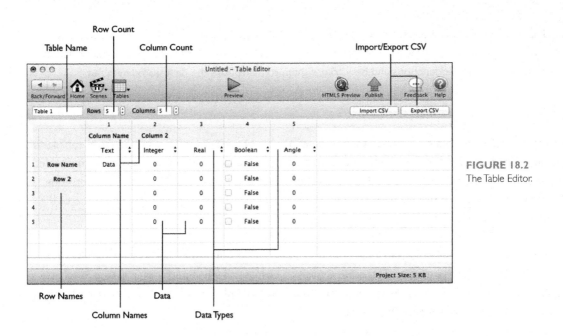

FIGURE 18.2
The Table Editor.

1. **Table name:** Use this field to edit the name of the table.
2. **Row Count:** This is the number of rows in the table. Input a number of rows and the appropriate number of rows will be added to or deleted from the table. The arrow buttons can also be used to increase or decrease the number of rows in the table.
3. **Column Count:** This is the number of columns in the table. Update the number and the appropriate number of columns will be added to or deleted from the table. The arrow buttons can also be used to increase or decrease the number of columns in the table.

4. **Import CSV/Export CSV:** Use these buttons to import data from a CSV file or export the current data as a CSV file.

5. **Column Names:** The top entry of each column can contain a column name. These column names can be used in behaviors to reference the column.

6. **Row Names:** The leftmost entry of a row can contain a row name. The row name can be used in behaviors to reference the row.

7. **Data Types:** Each column can contain any of the five data types Gamesalad supports: text, integer, real, boolean, and angle. Use the drop-down menu to choose the data type for each column in the table.

8. **Data:** This is the actual data of the table. Double-click a cell to edit its contents.

Note: CSV Files

A Comma Separated Value (CSV) file stores data in a plain-text format. Each row of data is followed by a line break and a comma separates each column of data. A CSV file is a simple file format that can be imported and exported by many applications.

Tip: Column and Row Names

While column and row names are not required, it is good practice to name them with relevant names. As the amount of data in a table grows, it will be extremely helpful to know exactly what each column and row represents. These names can also be referenced when creating behaviors.

Exercise 31

Top Ten High Scores

In this exercise, you'll create a table that could be used to organize, save, and display a list of high scores.

1. Create a new Gamesalad project for any platform and navigate to the Tables Tab.
2. Use the **Plus (+)** button to create a new Table and name it "TABLE-HighScores."
3. **Double-Click** the Table to open its Table Editor and change the number of rows to 10.
4. Name column 1, the only column, "Scores" and choose Integer as the data type.
5. Name the rows following this structure: "First," "Second," "Third," etc.
6. When you are done, the file should look like Figure 18.3 and is ready for use as a high score list.
7. **Save** the file from this exercise. You'll use it again later in this chapter.

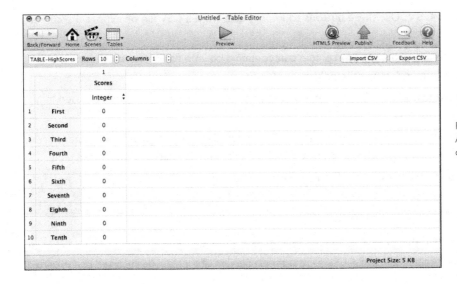

FIGURE 18.3
A table created to keep track of the top 10 high scores.

Table Related Behaviors

Gamesalad has several table related behaviors; a few of the most commonly used are described below:

» **Add/Remove Row:** With this behavior, you are able to add or remove rows from the selected table. Rows can be added to or removed from the beginning or end of a table. You can choose the row number (at index) that should be added or removed.

» **Change Table Value:** Use this behavior to change the value of a cell within a table. If the data types of the column and the value that is being changed don't match, the change will be ignored.

» **Copy Table:** This behavior is used to completely replace the contents of one table (A) with another table (B). Any data currently contained in the destination table (B) will be eliminated when the source table (A) is copied into it.

» **Save Table:** This saves the current data of the table to the device for later use. Saving tables is not supported in the Gamesalad Arcade.

Tip: Loading Tables

There is no need to specifically load table data, once a table is saved to memory it will always be available for use while the application is running.

Exercise 32

Changing Tables with Behaviors

In this exercise, you'll experiment with using behaviors to dynamically update a table.

1. Open the file you created for the previous exercise, navigate to the Initial Scene, and create a new empty Actor named "table display."

2. Open the Actor Editor and Drag a Display Text Behavior to the Behaviors List. Use the Expression Editor to create an Expression that reads (see Figure 18.4):

    tableRowCount(game.TABLE-HighScores)

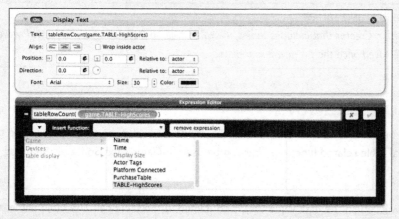

FIGURE 18.4
The completed Display Text Behavior.

3. To create the Expression above, you'll first need to insert the Function:
    tableRowCount(table)

4. Then **Select** the word "table" from the Formula and use the Attribute Browser to select:
    game.TABLE-HighScores

5. Finally, change the Display Text Color to Black.

6. Return to the Stage, add the Actor to the Stage, and Preview the scene. You will see the number 10 displayed in the Actor. This is the current number of Rows contained in the table named "HighScores."

Next, you'll use a table behavior to add more rows to the table. As you add the rows, the number displayed in the actor will increase as well.

7. Open the "table display" Actor Editor and add a Rule to the list of Behaviors.
8. Create a condition in the Rule that reads:
   Actor receives event » mouse button » is » down
9. Nest an Add/Remove Row Behavior in the Rule and set it up to read:
   Table: TABLE-HighScores
10. Preview the scene and **Click** the Mouse Button. Each time the button is pressed, a new row is added to the table and the number displayed in the actor increases by 1.
11. **Save** this file for use in the next exercise.

Note: Gamesalad Creator and Tables

When previewing a game within Creator that includes tables, the tables will update during game play. However, any data changes will not be saved once the preview is completed.

Table Related Functions

In the previous exercise, you used one of the table related functions to display the row count of the table, there are several additional table related functions that can be used in Gamesalad. Some of the most common are:

» **tableCellValue:** This will return the data value that is contained in the table cell. The table name, and row and column numbers, indicate which table cell to retrieve the data from.
» **tableMergeValues:** This will merge a range of rows or columns from the named table and return the merged value.
» **tableSearch:** This will search a named table's rows or columns for a user-established value and return its location in the table.

When choosing any of the table functions, you will be presented with a partial formula. Some of the data will need to be manually entered, through the Attributes Browser, to complete the function. For example, when adding a tableCellValue function to a behavior, you'll see the following formula in the Expression Editor:

tableCellValue(table,row,col)

To complete this function, you'll need to replace the word "table" with the table name you want to retrieve the data from. You then need to indicate the "row" and "column" where the cell is located. While each table function asks for slightly different information, they all follow this same basic format.

Exercise 33

Updating Table Data Values

In this exercise, you will use a function to update the value of a table cell.

1. **Open** the file you created in the previous exercise and **Open** the table display Actor Editor.
2. Update the Text Field of the Display Text Behavior to read:
   tableCellValue(game.TABLE-HighScores,"Fifth",1)
3. **Delete** the Add/Remove Row Behavior from the Rule and replace it with a Change Table Value Behavior that reads:
   Table: game.TABLE-HighScores » Row: 5 » Column: 1 » Value: 10
4. The Behavior List of the Actor should look like Figure 18.5.

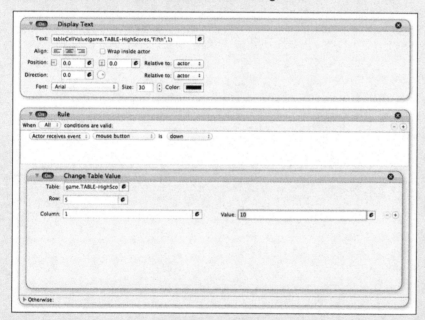

FIGURE 18.5
A behavior list that will update the data in row 5 of the TABLE-HighScores table.

5. **Preview** the Scene. When you click the mouse button, the value of the 5th row of column 1 will update from 0 to 10.

Note: Row and Column Names

In behaviors, rows and columns can be referred to by their names OR their numbers. As you may have noticed in the previous exercise, the row indicator in the tableCellValue function was referenced by its name "Fifth." The same row was referred to in the change table value behavior by its number, 5.

Summary

You spent the past chapter learning about tables in Gamesalad. You learned what tables are and what they can be used for in your games. You learned about some of the table related behaviors and practiced using some of them during this hour's exercises. Finally, you learned about table functions and how to manipulate data using them.

Chapter 19
Game Polish

In This Chapter You Will Learn:

» How to polish a game

» How to playtest a game

» How to polish game audio

» How to polish a game's GUI

» How to create a consistent graphic style

In this chapter, you will learn all about what it means to polish a video game. You'll learn how to playtest the project and learn what to watch for during the testing phase. Next, you will learn what can be done to polish the sound effects and soundtrack of the game. Afterwards, you will learn how to polish a game's GUI so it feels natural to the player. Finally, you will learn how to make sure the game follows a consistent graphic style.

Game Polish

Game polish is a very subjective term that will likely be defined somewhat differently by just about anybody you talk to in the video game industry. What most definitions of polish have in common is that polish is the part of a game's development that usually takes place toward the end of the project.

Polishing a game is all about fixing any small issues that arise during playtesting, adding small features, performing code and behavior optimizations, cleaning up graphic elements, and making sure the art style is consistent. Polish can vary by discipline. For a sound designer, it may be resampling audio and recompressing it; however, for an artist, it may be adding a bit more detail to a character or animation. If you are a sole indie developer or part of a very small team, you'll likely be doing most of the polishing yourself.

It's important to allow enough time in the game's development for a specific "polish phase." Polish has been referred to as the last 10-15% of your project that can be the most difficult to "get through." This last 10% of a project can often feel like it takes as long to complete as the first 90% of the project.

Playtesting

As I mentioned early in the book, you should be playtesting throughout the entire game development process. As the end of development approaches and you begin to anticipate the final release of all your hard work and time, don't lose sight of playtesting. Part of the polish phase should certainly include returning to the list of bugs or improvements that you had intended to make during development. Each bug and improvement should be thoroughly tested, making sure they have been corrected or added as planned. It's very easy to lose sight of a small detail while trying to track down and fix multiple bugs or features. So keep a list and try to keep the process organized.

Don't rely on only the development team's experience while playtesting. The more input that can be gathered on the game the better. If possible, enlist friends and family during the testing phase and even consider using Apples TestFlight service to help with the process if you are developing for iOS.

It may not be practical to ship a game with no bugs at all, but that should be the goal of the testing phase. Once the game is released to the masses, players will likely try to do things with your games, characters, and puzzles that you never imagined—certainly some previously unknown bugs will crop up. But anything that is found before the game is released should be corrected.

Game Audio

For many indie developers, it seems like audio is often an afterthought that is sometimes "thrown in" at the end of development. Most developers don't do this on purpose; they are just so busy working on the rest of the project that audio sometimes suffers. It is critical to remember that audio contributes a lot to the gaming experience. The right audio can totally change a game's mood and feel while poor audio, or no audio at all, can really bring an otherwise good game down.

There are a lot of opportunities to use audio in a game. Certainly there are the obvious uses for sounds and music; a soundtrack, button clicks, jumping sounds, gunshots, etc. But there are also a lot of less obvious uses for audio that are sometimes overlooked. Nearly every object that the player interacts with has the opportunity to bring more life to the game through audio. For example, when a gun fires, there will be the main shot sound, but also consider adding the sound of bullet shells hitting the ground or the sound of the gun reloading to add another layer to the audio experience. If the game world is a forest, consider adding ambient sounds of crickets chirping or birds singing to add a feeling of more life in the forest. If the game is a horror game, the sounds of distant screams or roaring monsters could go a long way toward intensifying the player's fear level.

Note: Ambient Sound

Ambient sound is another more technical term for background noise. Background noise is any sound other than the primary audio source.

Audio is an important part of the video game experience and should be given the attention it deserves.

The Graphical User Interface (GUI)

There is a whole section in this book dedicated to creating a Graphical User Interface (GUI), but it is important enough to mention again. Even if you and your testers are satisfied with your game's GUI, don't be afraid to view it one last time with a very critical eye. A GUI is typically on-screen during every level of a game. Even as the backgrounds and settings change, the GUI may not. For this reason, you should be positive the game's GUI is as clean, simplified, and optimized as possible.

A good GUI should only include information that is immediately relevant to the player and anything that is not critical to the game's action can be either removed or moved to another screen. Each game type will have its own critical elements that must be displayed at all times, but some examples are: a player's life, on-screen controls, ammunition count, and a level map. If you decide to rearrange your game's GUI and move some elements to another screen, a good candidate for that is often the pause screen. However, if there is a lot of extra information that needs to be displayed, you'll likely want to create a special screen to display it all.

A GUI can often benefit from some additional animation or effects as well. The areas of information could move into place when the level first loads, buttons could animate with different states (normal, hover, and active), and life meters could change color as the player's health increases and decreases. The options really are endless.

Graphic Style

Every game has a certain graphic style—the style of artwork used for the game graphics. Certainly this style should be chosen at the beginning of the project and not the end. But there are often so many assets that need to be created that they are created at different times, by different people. It is critical to review all the graphic elements used in a game during the polish phase and make sure they are all fit the same graphic style.

Most successful games don't mix art styles, but instead have one continuous style throughout all of the game's screens; splash screens, game play screens, credits screens, etc. This same art style usually extends to the game's website and marketing materials as well. There is no single art style that every game should use. Instead, there is an almost endless list of art styles to choose from, including:

Pixel Art Style

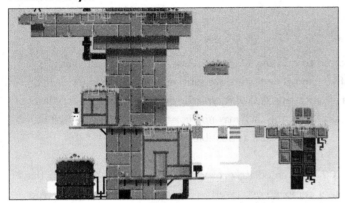

FIGURE 19.1
Pixel art graphics from the popular indie game Fez.

Cartoon Art Style

FIGURE 19.2
Cartoon art graphics from the Angry Birds series of games. Note that the characters, backgrounds and GUI are all created in the same cartoon style to maintain a consistent graphic look.

Sketch Art Style

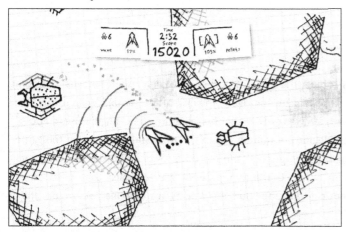

FIGURE 19.3
Sketch art graphics from the game SketchFighter 4000 Alpha.

Pre-rendered 3D Art Style

FIGURE 19.4
Pre-rendered 3D art graphics from the Donky Kong Country series of games.

The art style chosen for a game should be something that enhances the game's feel and mood, but most importantly, it should be consistently used throughout the entire game. If you play any of the games used as examples above, you will see that even though the art style of each game is very different, they have each used their chosen style consistently. If you choose to create your game play screens and characters in a pixel art style, you shouldn't create your menus and splash screens as pre-rendered 3D art. Make sure every element in your game is created in a consistent art style for the entire project.

Over Polish

It's possible to "over polish" a game. In every project there is a certain point of diminishing returns (the point at which changes you make will have very little effect on the overall quality of the game). While it can be hard to tell when you have reached that point, always try to weigh the effect of the change you are about to make or feature you are about to add and decide if it will be worth the time and effort when the game is complete. Certainly fixing a game-breaking bug is important and the time should be taken to correct it, but endlessly tweaking a special effect may not be worth it if that is the only bit of polish that is stopping the game from being released. It is a judgment call, but one you should be aware of while you are polishing your projects.

There are a lot of ways games can be polished. Every game has some common elements, but there will likely be some specific to each project as well. The subjects discussed in this chapter are common among just about any game project. But keep in mind this is not an exhaustive list. There will likely be some elements specific to your own games that should be tweaked and polished before publishing that are not mentioned here.

Summary

In the last chapter, you learned all about game polish and how to make sure a game is the best it can be. You learned about playtesting games and how to polish their audio and graphical user interfaces. Finally, you learned the importance of having a consistent art style.

Chapter 20
Game 4—Geometry Runner

In This Chapter You Will Learn

» How to design the game "Geometry Runner"

» How to build the actors for "Geometry Runner"

» How to create the game world for "Geometry Runner"

In this chapter, you will create an endless runner style game similar to the popular game "Geometry Dash." Just like the other games, the basic building blocks, art and sounds, are provided and you will add all of the behaviors needed to complete the project. You will begin by examining the game concept, rules, and requirements. Afterwards, you will build the game world and add the actors and actions to make everything work.

Note: Project Files

The starter project files and a finished version of the Geometry Runner game, in case you get stuck, are in the Book Assets for Chapter 20.

Game Concept

The concept of Geometry Runner is to avoid obstacles and keep your pixel moving on-screen throughout the entire game level. If the pixel hits an obstacle or stops moving, it will explode and the player will restart at the beginning of the level.

Game Rules

» The player's pixel will constantly move to the right

» If the pixel hits an obstacle or stops moving, it will explode

» Clicking the mouse button will cause the pixel to jump and rotate

» The players pixel character will remain in the center of the screen and all objects will move toward it from the right

Game Requirements

» The game will be built using the iPhone 6 Landscape platform

» 2 custom game attributes will be used to monitor win and loss conditions

» 9 actors for the player and level elements are needed

» Particle effects will be used for various special effects

» A soundtrack is needed

Game Setup

To start the project, open up the file named "Geometry Runner-Starter" located in the Assets Folder for Chapter 20. Take a moment to look through the project and note that is has been set up using the iPhone 6 landscape platform. There is one scene, seven images, and one audio file provided in the project. Take special note that in the scene tab, the width of the scene has been extended to 5,336 pixels. This long scene is what will allow the game to scroll from the right during game play.

Note: Resolution Independence

Make sure resolution independance is activated on the project info screen.

Game Attributes

Since you will need two game level attributes to monitor the game's win and loss conditions, let's set those up first:

1. Navigate to the Attributes Tab in the Inspector Palette and add two Boolean Attributes.
2. Name one "win" and one "lose" and leave them both unchecked so they start as False.

Game Actors

The first step in creating the game will be to create all of the required actors.

1. Select all of the images in the Images Tab and **Drag** them into the Actors Tab to create actors for each image.
2. Use the **Plus (+)** button to add two more empty Actors to the Project. Name one actor "goal" and the other "you win!".

Many of the actors in the this game will not have any behaviors applied to them. They will just need some initial set up in their Attributes and they will be set for use in the game. Follow the steps outlined below for the actor's named floor, background, block, half-block, and spike.

3. Open each Actor. Zero is the physics settings and uncheck the Moveable option.

4. In each actor's Graphics Settings, choose the Tile option for the Horizontal and Vertical Wrap.

5. Navigate to the Actors Tab from the Home Screen and create a new Tag named "floor."

6. **Drag** the actor's floor, block, and half-block into the "floor" tag (see Figure 20.1).

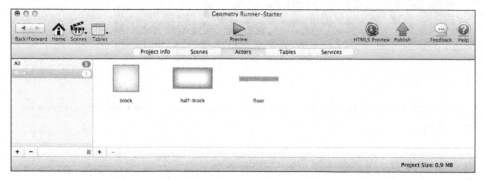

FIGURE 20.1
The actors that tagged as "floor".

Since the background and floor actors don't need any behaviors, you should go ahead and place them on the stage so you will have an area to test the other actors on.

7. Place the background actor on the Stage and **Drag** its adjustment handles so it fills the entire Scene.

8. Place the floor actor toward the bottom of the Stage and use its adjustment handles to stretch it to fit the entire width of the Scene (see Figure 20.2).

Tip: Numerical Placement

If you don't want to manually drag the handles to place the background and floor actors on the stage you can place them numerically by placing them on the stage and updating their postions and sizes like so:

Background: *Postion (2668, 187.5), Size (5336, 375)*

Floor: *Position (2668, 0), Size (5336, 82)*

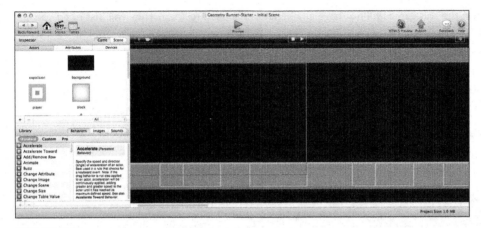

FIGURE 20.2
The background and floor actors placed on the stage.

Most of the action for this game is going to be controlled by the player actor. So let's start by creating its behaviors and get it working.

1. Open the player Actors Editor and update its Physics properties to:
   Friction 0 » Bounciness 0

2. Add two Real Attributes to the list and name them "myRotation" and "previousX." Leave them both set to zero.

3. Add a Collide Behavior to the player and set it up to read:
   Bounce when colliding with: » actor with tag » floor

4. Add an Accelerate Behavior and make it read:
   Direction 270 » Acceleration 1,000 » Relative to: scene

Return to the Stage and place the player actor anywhere on-screen above the floor actor. **Preview** the game and the player should drop until it hits the floor actor, where it should come to a rest. The next step is to get the player moving on-screen. To do this, return to the player Actor Editor and:

1. Add a Rule to the players list of behaviors and create two conditions that read:
   Attribute » game.win » is » false
   Attribute » game.lose » is » false

2. Nest a Constrain Attribute Behavior in the Rule and set it to read:
   Constraint Attribute: » self.Motion.Linear Velocity.X » To: » 300

3. Place a copy of the Constraint Attribute Behavior into the Otherwise section of the Rule and change the number 300 to 0 (see Figure 20.3).

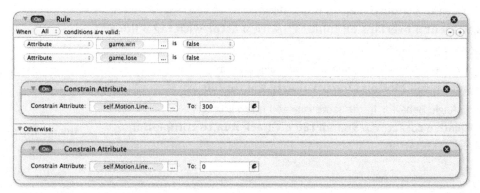

FIGURE 20.3
The rule that will control the players movement.

4. Add a Control Camera Behavior to the list of behaviors.
5. Return to the Stage and place the player Actor in the exact center of the Stage, resting on the floor Actor.
6. Use the Camera Control Mode Icon to activate the Camera Control Handles. **Drag** them both to the center of the stage (see Figure 20.4).

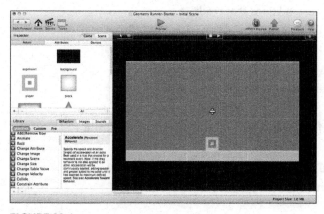

FIGURE 20.4
The camera tracking zone adjusted to be closed on the center of the stage.

Preview the scene and the player will now move along the empty level to the right. If you let it play long enough, it will pass the scene boundary on the right and disappear off of the screen. Now that the player is correctly moving through the scene, let's add the ability to jump and add a nice particle trail effect.

1. Open the Actor Editor for the player and add a new Rule to the list. Give this rule three conditions that read:

    Actor receives event » mouse button » is » down

    Actor receives event » overlaps or collides » with » actor with tag » floor

    Attribute » game.win » is » false

2. Nest a Change Attribute Behavior in the Rule and make it read:

    Change Attribute » self.Motion.Linear Velocity.Y » To: 400

3. Nest a Rotate to Angle Behavior in the same rule and make it read:

    Angle: 270 » Relative to: actor » Speed: 180 » Check Run to completion » Check Stops on destination

---

Note: Jumping Routine

This jump rule may seem a little complex so let's examine its functionality more closely. The conditions will allow the player to jump only when the mouse button is clicked AND the player is touching any actor tagged as a floor AND the game has not been won yet. When a jump is allowed, the player will be pushed up into the air with the change attribute behavior and at the same time, the player will be rotated from 0 to 270° because of the rotate to angle behavior.

---

4. Add another Rule to the list and create three conditions that read:

    Actor receives event » overlaps or collides » with » actor with tag » floor

    Attribute » game.win » is » false

    Attribute » game.lose » is » false

5. Nest a Particles Behavior in the rule and set its tabs up as follows:

    a. Spawn Rate:

    Number of Particles: 100 » Particle Startup Time: 1.5 » Particle Lifetime: 1

    b. Velocity/Position:

    Emitter Offset: X: random(-30,-20) Y: random(-30,-20) » Direction: 90 » Relative to Scene » Speed: random(5,25)

    c. Size:

    Size: random(7,15) » Size changes to » Target Size: 0 » Duration: 1

    d. Color:

    Choose any color you like and set it to change to white with a duration of .5.

    e. There are no settings for Rotation and Image.

Preview the scene. Now, as the player moves along the floor, it should create a particle trail. Pressing the mouse button will cause the player to jump and rotate. It will also cause the particle trail to pause while the player is in the air.

The next step in creating the hero's behaviors is to get it to interact with the obstacles that will be in the game. The player will need to interact with spikes and blocks. To create the spike interaction:

1. Add a new Rule to the player's list of Behaviors and create a condition that reads:
    Actor receives event » overlaps or collides » with » actor of type » spike
2. Nest a Change Attribute Behavior in the Rule and make it read:
    Change Attribute » game.lose » To: true

This Rule will flag the player as dead when it collides with a spike, but you still need to tell the game what to do when the player dies. To do that, follow these steps:

Note: What is a Flag?

Flag is a term that is often used in conjunction with boolean attributes. If a boolean attribute is true it can be refered to as being flagged or being flagged as true.

---

1. Create a new Rule in the player and name it "Lose." Create two conditions for this rule that read:
    Attribute » game.lose » is » true
    Attribute » game.win » is » false
2. Nest three Behaviors in the rule: an Interpolate Behavior, a Spawn Actor Behavior, and a Timer. Make sure and nest the three attributes in that order from top to bottom.
3. Set the Interpolate Behavior up to read:
    Interpolate Attribute: self.Color.Alpha » To: 0.0 » Duration: 0.2
4. For the Spawn Actor Behavior, choose the "explosion" Actor from the Actor Drop-Down Menu.
5. Set the Timer up to read:
    After » 2 seconds
6. Nest a Reset Game Attribute in the Timer.

To test what you have done in the last several steps, add a spike somewhere to the right of the player and **Preview** the game. Once the player hits the spike, the game will stop and reset. You'll notice that no explosion was triggered; in fact, a weird circle was placed on-screen instead. This is because you have not created the explosion effect yet, you'll do that later in this chapter.

There are three more routines that need to be added to the player to complete its behaviors list. First, you'll add the "win" trigger:

1. Open the player's Actor Editor and add a new Rule to the list. Name this rule "Win."
2. Create a condition for the Rule that reads:
    Actor receives event » overlaps or collides » with » actor of type » goal
3. Nest a Change Attribute in the Rule and make it read:
    Change Attribute: game.win » To: true

Every game can benefit from a soundtrack. To add one to this game:

1. **Drag** the audio file from the Sounds Tab and **Drop** it in the player's Behavior list to automatically add a Play Music Behavior.
2. Check the Loop check box so the song will start over again once the end of the song is reached.

Finally, the last thing you'll need to check for in the player's behaviors is if the player hits the edge of a block and stops moving. If that is the case the player should be destroyed. The obvious way to create this event may be to use a rule that checks to see if the player "overlaps or collides" with a block. However, since the player needs the blocks to act like a floor when the player is on top of it, you won't be able to use the obvious solution in this case.

1. Add a Timer Behavior to the player's Behaviors and set it up to read:
    Every » 0.05 seconds » check Run to Completion
2. Nest a Change Attribute Behavior in the Timer and make it read:
    Change Attribute: self.previousX » To: self.PositionX
3. Nest another Timer Behavior below the Change Attribute Behavior and set it to read:
    After » 0.02 seconds » check Run to Completion
4. Nest a Rule in this Timer and create a condition that reads:
    Attribute » self.previousX » equals (=) » self.PositionX
5. Nest a Change Attribute Behavior in this Rule and make it read:
    Change Attribute: game.lose » To: true

The finished timer behavior should look like Figure 20.5.

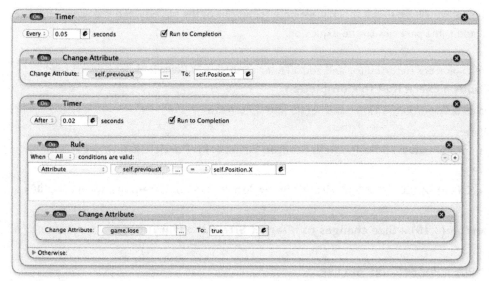

FIGURE 20.5
The completed Timer Behavior.

Note: Creative Solutions

While Gamesalad has many built-in behaviors and actions, it's important to remember that the developers can't predict every possible situation. Once you learn enough about how the built-in components work, you can combine them in a way to create some very complex systems. For example, the timer behavior you just set up records the player's X position every 0.05 seconds and then compares that value to its current X position. If that value remains equal after 0.02 seconds, that means the player has stopped moving and the player should lose.

Now that the hero's behaviors are complete, let's move on to the rest of the game's actors, starting with the explosion. Open the Actor Editor for the explosion actor and:

1. Start by adding an Interpolate Behavior to the list of Behaviors. Set this up to read:
    Interpolate Attribute: self.Color.Alpha » To: 0.0 » Duration: 0.4
2. Add another Interpolate Behavior and make it read:
    Interpolate Attribute: self.Size.Width » To: 512 » Duration: 0.4
3. Add a third Interpolate Behavior and make it read:
    Interpolate Attribute: self.Size.Height » To: 512 » Duration: 0.4
4. Combine these three interpolate behaviors into a Group named "shock wave."

Preview the game and you'll see that a shock wave now grows out of the player when it collides with the spike. Next, you'll add some particles to the explosion.

1.   Return to the explosions Actor Editor and add a Timer to the list of Behaviors. Set it up to read:
     For 0.4 seconds » check Run to Completion

2.   Nest a Particles Behavior in the Timer and set its tabs up to read:

     a.   Spawn Rate:
          Number of Particles: 200 » Particle Startup Time: 0.4 » Particle Lifetime: 2

     b.   Velocity/Position:
          Emitter Offset: X 0.0 » Y 0.0 » Direction: random(0,359) » Speed: random(200,400)

     c.   Size:
          Size: random(3,10) » Size changes to » Target Size: 0.0 » Duration: 2

     d.   Color:
          Choose any color settings you like

     e.   Rotation:
          Angular Velocity: random(200,800)

3.   To complete the explosion, add another Timer Behavior at the bottom of the list and set it up to read:
     After 2 seconds

4.   Nest a Destroy Behavior in the Timer Behavior.

Note: Timers and Particles

Particle behaviors are often combined with timer behaviors to control how often or at what interval the particles should be triggered. For the explosion you just created, a timer behavior is used to trigger the particle effect only one time.

Tip: Destroying Actors

Since the explosion actor's alpha value was reduced to 0, it appears to have been removed from the stage. However, it will actually still be there, you just won't be able to see it anymore. All actors on the stage have an impact on the game's performance, even if you can't see them, so it's important to use a destroy behavior to actually remove the actor from the stage. This will help keep the game running as smoothly as possible.

Next, open the Actor Editor for the goal Actor and add a Particles Behavior to its Behaviors list. Take special note that unlike the explosions particle effect, the goals particle effect is *not* enclosed in a timer behavior. Because of that this particle effect will run continuously throughout the game. Set the Particle Behaviors tabs up to read:

1. Spawn Rate:
    Number of Particles: 100 » Particle Startup Time: 10 » Particle Lifetime: 10
2. Velocity/Position:
    Emitter Offset: » X: random(-(self.Size.Width /2),(self.Size.Width /2)) »
    Y: random(-(self.Size.Height /2),(self.Size.Height /2)) » Direction: 90 »
    Speed: random(5,30)
    (see Figure 20.6)

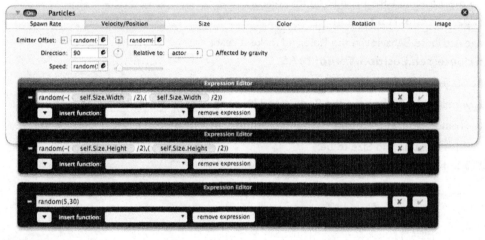

FIGURE 20.6
The Velocity/Position Tab of the completed Particles Behavior.

3. Size:
    Size: random(3,10) » Size changes to » Target Size: 0.0 » Duration: 10
4. Color:
    Choose any color settings you like.
5. Rotation and Image have no settings.
6. Finally expose the Color Settings for the goal Actor and update the Alpha setting to:
    Alpha: 0.1

Tip: Actor Width and Height

In step 2 (above), you directly accessed the actor's width and height settings within the expression. Doing this allows you to create a particle effect that will correctly work with a goal actor of any size.

To complete all of the actor's behaviors, open the Actor Editor for the Actor named "you win!"

1. Change the Actor's color to Black and update the Alpha value to 0.75.
2. Add a Display Text Behavior to the Actor and set it up to read:
    Text: You Win! » Size: 50
3. Add a Change Attribute Behavior and set it up to read:
    Change Attribute: self.Position.Y » To: -375
4. Add a Rule to the list and create a condition that reads:
    Attribute » game.win » is » true
5. Nest a Change Attribute Behavior in the Rule and make it read:
    Change Attribute: self.Position.Y » To: 187.5
6. Return to the Stage and navigate to the Layers Tab of the Scene Palette.
7. Add a new Layer named "Win" above the Background Layer and uncheck scrollable (see Figure 20.7).
8. Add the Actor named "you win!" to this layer and **Double-Click** it to open its Attributes Palette.
9. Update this actor's Position and Size to be:
    Position (333.5, 187.5) » Size (667,375).

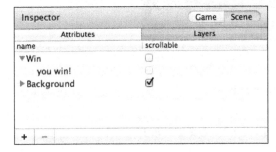

FIGURE 20.7
The Layers Tab showing the "Win" and "Background" layers.

All of the actors you'll need for the game are now complete. The final step is to build a playable level.

Level Building

This exercise is going to be a little different than the others. I am going to leave the actual building of the game level up to you. Once the actors have been created and their behaviors have been added, you can use the pieces to create any level layout you'd like. Of course, the file provided for reference has a fully complete and working level—you can copy that one if you like or create something completely new and different.

Note: Level Building

With an action game like the one you are creating, the construction of the level(s) can take a long time. The spacing of each object is critical and needs to be tested and retested throughout the development. Since the speed of the game and the jumping action of the player will be constant, it will be the construction of the actual level elements that make each level hard or easy to complete.

There are a few things to keep in mind when you are creating a game level:

1. The only actor that should be placed on the Win layer is the "you win!" actor.
2. All of the game's other elements and actors should be placed on the background layer.
3. Every level needs a goal actor at the end for the player to collide with and complete the level.
3. The obstacle actors and the goal actor have all been created so that you can resize them as needed and they work as expected.

Good luck and most importantly, have fun while building your first custom game level!

Summary

In the last chapter, you learned how to create an endless runner style game. You started by reviewing the game's rules and requirements. Afterwards, you created the actors needed for the game and added the behaviors each actor needed to perform its job in the game. You then added a music soundtrack to the game and finally you created a game level on your own.

Chapter 21
Mobile Development

In This Chapter You Will Learn

» How to configure your development environment for mobile development

» How to test games on a mobile device

» How to save and load data on the device

» How to set up accelerometer-based controls

» How to detect and track multiple touch events at once

Since the launch of the Apple App Store in 2008, games have been one of the most downloaded categories of apps for iOS devices. The same holds true for the Android App Stores. With Gamesalad, it's easy to develop games for use on just about any mobile device available today. In this chapter, you'll learn how to configure your development environment for mobile publishing. Next, you will learn how to test games on a mobile device. Afterwards, you will learn how to save and load data to/from the mobile device. Finally, you will learn how to create controls for games on a mobile device using the accelerometer and multi-touch input.

Note: Gamesalad Free vs. Paid

As a user of the free version of Gamesalad, you are able to publish to the Apple App Store. This chapter's lesson will focus specifically on publishing for Apples iOS devices. If you are using the paid version of Gamesalad, you will also be able to publish to Android, Amazon, Kindle, and Tizen devices. Many of the subjects covered in this chapter apply to non-Apple devices as well.

Configuring Your Environment

Before you are able to publish and distribute games to mobile devices, you'll need to set up your development environment. The first step in that process is signing up with each app store that you want to distribute games through. In order to sell, or give away, your games on the Apple App Store, you'll need to sign up with Apple to become a Certified Apple Developer.

Note: The Cost of Developing

At the time of this writing, the cost of signing up to be a Certified Apple Developer is $99 (USD) per year. If you plan to sell your games through their app store, Apple will take 30% and pay you the remaining 70% of the game's income. Of course, if you give your games away for free, there is no income to split with Apple.

After signing up to be a Certified Apple Developer, you'll also need to:

1. Install Xcode and Application Loader on your Macintosh. Both are free and available from Apple.
2. Set up a development certificate.
3. Create a distribution profile.
4. Set up your device for testing.
5. Test your game either in Gamesalad's viewer or as an ad-hoc build.
6. Submit the game(s) to the Apple App Store.

While the specifics of each of those steps are beyond the scope of this book, don't worry; there are lots of resources available online from Gamesalad, Apple and other sources to help ease the process. The first time you go through the process of testing and publishing to any mobile platform, it may seem overwhelming; however, as you get more practice, the process will become second nature.

Gamesalad offers an online "cookbook" that outlines each step needed to publish to the Apple App Store. This is located at the URL below:

https://help.gamesalad.com/hc/en-us/sections/2004421 I6-3-Apple-Publishing

Apple's online developer site can be found at this URL:

https://developer.apple.com/

Mobile Playtesting

It's already been discussed that you should always playtest games before you release them; this certainly applies to the mobile platforms as well. Once a game is ready to be tested on a mobile device, there are two options: The Gamesalad Viewer can be used or the game can be built as a full ad-hoc build and tested live on the device. In this chapter, you will learn how to use the Gamesalad Viewer to quickly test games on an Apple iDevice (iPod, iPhone, iPad).

Note: Testing Requirements

In order to test on a mobile device, you will, of course need to have a device to test on. If you don't currently have access to a device, you should still read through this chapter so you understand the process. Even without a mobile device, you can still create games for iDevices—you just won't personally be able to test your games on a device before publishing.

The Gamesalad Viewer is an app that is installed on the mobile device and is used to quickly test games as they are being developed. The viewer can be downloaded from Gamesalad's website at:

http://gamesalad.com/download/latest/ios-viewer

The viewer application will need to be installed on each device that games will be tested on. To install the Gamesalad Viewer, follow the instructions provided by Gamesalad at the URL below:

https://help.gamesalad.com/hc/en-us/articles/202036063-3-3-Prepping-your-device-to-use-the-GameSalad-Viewer

Once the viewer has been installed on your device and the device is turned on and on the same Wi-Fi network as the computer you are running Gamesalad Creator on, there will be a new icon displayed next the Preview button at the top of the window. (see Figure 21.1).

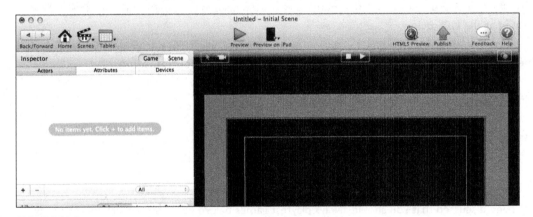

FIGURE 21.1
The "Preview on Device" menu has been added to the Gamesalad Creator window.

This new "Preview on device" button acts as a pull-down menu. With the viewer installed on an iPad, iPhone, and iPod, you'll be able to choose which device you'd like to preview the game on.

Tip: Viewer vs. Ad-hoc

The Gamesalad Viewer is great for a quick test while developing, but you should always test your games using a full ad-hoc build as well before you publish any games through the App Store. The viewer is an emulator that runs on the device; because it is emulation, sometimes things will not work the same as doing a full ad-hoc build. An ad-hoc build takes more time, but it produces a 100% native application.

Note: Certified Apple Developer

To install the Gamesalad Viewer (or any custom software) on an iDevice, you need to be a Certified Apple Developer. If you have not signed up with Apple, do so now or you will not be able to complete the exercise below.

Exercise 34

The Gamesalad Viewer

If you have a device to test on, follow these steps to create and test your first app using the Gamesalad Viewer.

1. Make sure you have downloaded and installed Gamesalad Viewer App on your mobile device.
2. Create a new portrait project whose platform type matches your mobile device. For example, if you plan on testing on an iPad, create a project using the iPad portrait platform.
3. Navigate to the Stage and create an empty Actor named "Square."
4. Place a copy of the Actor at the center of the stage.
5. Open and Run the Gamesalad Viewer on your device.
6. Once the Preview on Device Button appears in Creator, choose your device from the Drop-Down menu.
7. After a moment, the screen in Creator will change to the "remote preview screen" (see Figure 21.2) and the project will be displayed on your mobile device.
8. Save this project for later use in this chapter.

This project is not "playable." There is no interaction, but you should see the square actor positioned in the center of your devices screen.

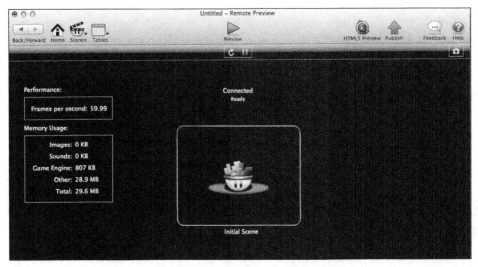

FIGURE 21.2
The "Remote Preview Screen" is displayed while your project is running in the Gamesalad Viewer App.

Note: The Remote Preview Screen

This screen displays lots of useful data about your project while it is playing on your device. It will track the projects performance, measured in frames per second, and display a lot of useful memory usage statistics.

Saving and Loading Data

There will be many times when you need to save and load data in the games you have created. You may simply want to save a high score or you may create a complex RPG game that needs to save player stats, weapons, and location information. Gamesalad offers two different ways to save and load data.

Save and Load Behaviors

The Save and Load Behaviors are used to save and load one attribute value at a time. When using the save behavior, you'll need to indicate what attribute to save and you need to assign a specific save location as a key value (see Figure 21.3).

▼ On	Save Attribute	⊗
Attribute: [ ] [...]	Key: [ ] 𝑒	

FIGURE 21.3
The Save Behavior.

» **Attribute:** Use the Attribute Browser to choose which Attribute should be saved.

» **Key:** A key is a specific string of characters that is assigned to each individual save location. This key is used to identify the save file and is used to reload the data later using the Load Behavior. A key can be any string of characters you like.

To use the Load Behavior (see Figure 21.4), you will need to supply the same two pieces of information in reverse order. Data will be loaded from the Key location provided and will be placed into the Attribute indicated. Data loaded into an Attribute will replace the previous value that the Attribute held.

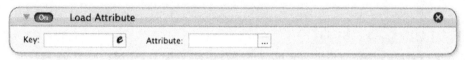

FIGURE 21.4
The Load Behavior.

While the save and load behaviors work great for small amounts of data, if there is a lot of information to keep track of, Tables are a more efficient option for saving and loading data.

Save Table

Using tables to save data takes a bit of pre-planning, but if there are large amounts of data to save, it's worth taking the time up front to plan for it.

Imagine for a moment that you are creating an RPG game and for your player character, you'll need to keep track of the following values: health, strength, armor, endurance, speed, and luck. You can, of course, create them as individual Attributes and save and load them one by one. However, it would be more efficient to plan ahead and create a table named "player stats" that contains all six values—you could then load them from the table as needed and save that table whenever any of the values change. To save a table during game play, trigger the Save Table Behavior (see Figure 21.5).

FIGURE 21.5
The Save Table Behavior.

Once triggered, the table indicated in the pull-down menu will be saved to the device. There is no need to reload table data. Once a table is saved, it is immediately available in the game to be read from or saved.

The save table behavior completely overwrites all of the original data in the table with any data that has been updated. Be careful not to accidently overwrite data you don't intend to.

Tip: Table Best Practice

It's common to create two tables for every set of data used in a game. For example, when creating the "player stats" table discussed above, create a second table called "player stats defaults." That way, if the "player stats" table ever needs to be reverted to its default values, the data from the "player stats defaults" table can be copied into the "player stats" table using a copy table behavior.

Accelerometer Control

Most mobile devices have an accelerometer built into them. An accelerometer measures the force of acceleration through movement or gravity. On a mobile device, the accelerometer is usually used to determine which way the screen is being held (portrait or landscape) and to measure the tilt of the device.

An accelerometer is able to detect changes on the X, Y, and Z-axis (see Figure 21.6).

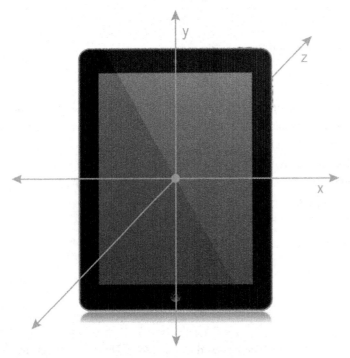

FIGURE 21.6
The accelerometers X, Y and Z axis.

The default axis for the accelerometer is when the device is located in the upright, portrait position as indicated in the figure above. If the device is rotated to the landscape position, the accelerometer data will need to be converted to the correct axis.

Exercise 35

Using the accelerometer

In this exercise, you'll add two behaviors to the square from the previous exercise to make it move using the accelerometer.

1. Open the previous exercise and open the Actor Editor for the square actor. If you didn't create the previous exercise for a portrait orientation, recreate it as a portrait project.

2. Add a Rule to the Actor and make its condition read:
   Attribute » game.Accelerometer.X » is greater than (>) » 0.1

3. Nest a Move Behavior in the rule and leave it set at its default values.

4. Copy the Rule and update the condition to read:
   Attribute » game.Accelerometer.X » is less than (>) » -0.1

5. Update the Move Behavior of this rule to read:
   Direction: 180

6. Use the Gamesalad Viewer to test this on your device and you'll see that when you tilt right and left, the square moves in the appropriate direction.

7. Rotate the device to a landscape orientation and you'll see, as mentioned above, that you no longer get the expected results because the axis has shifted.

8. Save this exercise for use in the next section.

Note: Accelerometer Attributes

The accelerometers X, Y, and Z Attributes are located in the devices section of the attribute browser (see Figure 21.7).

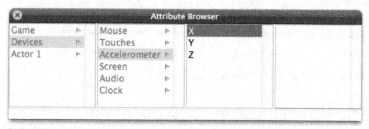

FIGURE 21.7
The accelerometer settings withing the devices section of the attribute browser.

Multi-Touch Control

Most mobile devices are primarily controlled by touch; through the capacitive screen, the device is able to detect multiple touches and the location of each touch. Gamesalad is able to detect up to eleven touches at one time. Keep in mind that even though Gamesalad is able to detect up to eleven touches, that does not mean every mobile device is able to detect that many touches. Different mobile devices from different manufactures are able to detect different numbers of touch events. In addition to detecting the number of touches, the specific X and Y location of each touch is tracked by Gamesalad as well.

The exact attribute names of each touch attribute can be found in the devices tab of the inspector palette (see Figure 21.8).

Inspector		Game Scene
Actors	Attributes	Devices
▶ Mouse		attributes
▼ Touches		attributes
Count	0	index
▼ Active		attributes
Touch 1	☐	boolean
Touch 2	☐	boolean
Touch 3	☐	boolean
Touch 4	☐	boolean
Touch 5	☐	boolean
Touch 6	☐	boolean
Touch 7	☐	boolean
Touch 8	☐	boolean
Touch 9	☐	boolean
Touch 10	☐	boolean
Touch 11	☐	boolean
▼ Touch 1		point
X	0	real
Y	0	real
▶ Touch 2		point

FIGURE 21.8
The Touches Attributes located in the Inspector Palette.

» **Count:** This is an integer number indicating the total number of touches currently on the screen.

» **Active:** This is a boolean value indicating the true or false state of each touch.

» **Touch–X/Y:** This is a real number indicating the X and Y coordinates of the touch.

By using these values, some very interesting controls and interactions can be created for games.

Exercise 36

Counting on Your Fingers

In this exercise, you will track and display the amount of touches on the device's screen.

1. Open the file from the previous exercise and open the Actor Editor for the square Actor.
2. Turn off or **Delete** the two Rules that were added during the previous exercise.
3. Add a Display Text Behavior to the list and update its color to Black.
4. Open the Expression Editor for the Text field and make it read:
   game.Touches.Count (see Figure 21.9)

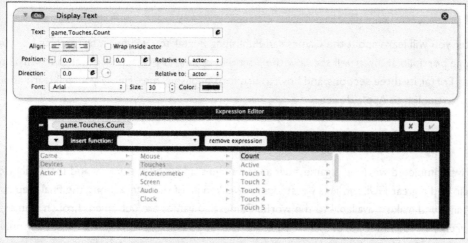

FIGURE 21.9
Adding Touches.Count to a Display Text Behavior.

5. Preview the project on your device using the Gamesalad Viewer and for each finger touched to the screen. The number displayed will increase by 1.

Summary

In this chapter, you discovered how to set up your development environment with mobile devices in mind and learned how to playtest games on your own device. You then learned how to save and load data to and from the device. Afterwards, you learned how to read the accelerometer and how to use it to control objects on-screen. Finally, you learned about multi-touch capacitive screens and how to track multiple touches at one time.

Chapter 22
Publishing

In This Chapter You Will Learn:

» How to log into your game portfolio

» How to use the Gamesalad Publishing Portal

» The requirements for Gamesalad Arcade publishing

» The requirements for publishing to Apple devices

In this chapter, you will learn about the Gamesalad Publishing Portal. You will begin by learning how to log into your game portfolio and you will see how the portfolio organizes projects. You will then learn about the Publishing Portal, its three sections, and how to use it to publish games. Finally, you will learn about the requirements to publish to Apple devices.

Publishing A Game

Once you have completed work on a game, built all the scenes, added all the actors and their behaviors, included audio and a great GUI, and finally tested and tweaked all of the interactions, the final step is to publish the game and make it available to the world. Gamesalad games are published through Gamesalad's publishing portal. The publishing portal is a website that is used to collect and organize all of your published projects. Through the publishing portal, you are able set up many of a game's default options and upload icons, screen shots, and even custom splash screens.

Project Portfolio

As part of the publishing portal, Gamesalad will build a portfolio of every project you have ever published. To view your portfolio, log into the Gamesalad website and choose Portfolio from the user menu (see Figure 22.1).

From this menu, you can also update your user profile and account settings and also review any purchases you have made through the Gamesalad Marketplace.

Once you have published a game, you'll be able to quickly navigate to its page (at the publishing portal) to review the game's settings, download the source file, or even delete the game from your portfolio.

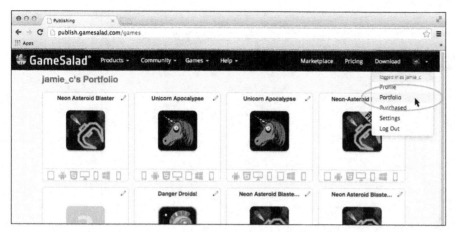

FIGURE 22.1
The portfolio menu option.

Publishing Portal

The publishing portal is divided into three main parts: the title, categories, and the details sections (see Figure 22.2).

Title Section

The title section is used to add a game's title and icon. Every game, regardless of the platform, must have a title and icon. The title and icon used in these fields will appear on the portfolio page.

Categories Section

The categories section lists various ad services and platforms that Gamesalad supports. Most of the platforms will have boxes (numbered in red) next to their name—these indicate the number of elements that MUST be completed in each platform's detail section in order for a project to be published on that platform.

Note: Platforms

The publishing portal lists all of the platforms that Gamesalad is able to publish to. Just because a platform is listed, it doesn't mean you'll be able to successfully publish to it. Publishing is limited by your member status (free vs. paid) and by how you have created the project within Creator.

FIGURE 22.2
The publishing portal interface.

Details Section

Based on the category chosen, the content of the details section will vary. In Figure 22.2 (above), the HTML5 platform, also known as the Gamesalad Arcade, is chosen so the details for that platform are requested. There are four red alerts listed at the top of the page—these four alerts correspond to the number in the red box next to the platform name in the categories section. Once these minimum requirements have been satisfied, the game is able to be published to the chosen platform.

Note: Online Backup

During the publishing process, Gamesalad archives a copy of the project file at the publishing portal. If a published game is ever deleted from your local hard drive, the project file can be downloaded from the Gamesalad Publishing Portal. (see Figure 22.3).

FIGURE 22.3
The download button on the publishing portal.

Exercise 37

Publish to the Gamesalad Arcade

In this exercise, you'll publish the Space Shooter game from chapter 11 to the Gamesalad Arcade. This exercise will use the files provided in the "space shooter images" folder in the Assets Folder for Chaper 22.

1. Open the space shooter game you completed in Chapter 11.
2. **Press** the Publish Button in the Creator window (see Figure 22.4).

FIGURE 22.4
The Publish button in Gamesalad Creator.

3. Gamesalad will upload the game project to the publishing portal and open your system's default browser.
4. From this window, you can either Publish as a New Game or Update an Existing Game. Choose "Publish as New Game" since this is the first time the game is being published. When choosing to update an existing game, the previous details entered in the publishing portal will be used as default settings for the updated game.
5. Choose the Arcade Platform in the categories section (left column). If that platform is not already exposed, **Click** the down arrow next to the Platform's heading to show the full list of platforms available.

6. In the title section, enter "Space Shooter" as the game title.

7. **Click** on the "Icon +" button and upload the icon provided for this exercise.

8. **Click** the **Save** button under the title and one of the red alerts should disappear. If the title needs to be edited once you have saved the settings, **Click** the pencil icon that will appear next to the title.

9. Enter a description in the Description field; this can be anything you like.

10. Next, **Click** the three "+ image" buttons in the Screen Shots section and upload the three screen shots provided for this exercise.

11. At this point, the requirements to publish have been met and the Publish button will become active (see Figure 22.5).

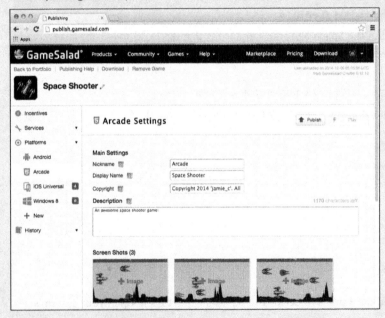

FIGURE 22.5
The completed information for the game to be published to the Gamesalad Arcade.

12. Before clicking the Publish button, review the rest of the information on the screen. While you don't have to make any edits in order to publish the game, it's a good idea to familiarize yourself with all the available options.

13. Once you have reviewed the screen, **Click** the **Publish** button and you will be presented with a message that your app is "queued for generation." At this point the remote Gamesalad servers are generating the app for you, the wait time at this stage will vary depending on how busy the servers are at the time of generation.

14. If the page does not reload automatically in a few minutes, force the page to reload by **Clicking** the reload button in your browser.

15. When you see a message indicating that the app is ready (see Figure 22.6) the publishing process is complete. Since the game has been published to the Arcade, you can ignore the message about signing the app. That message is intended for use when publishing for mobile devices.

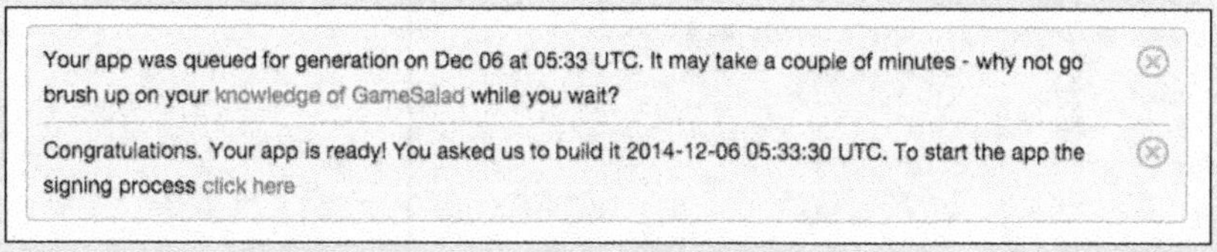

> Your app was queued for generation on Dec 06 at 05:33 UTC. It may take a couple of minutes - why not go ⊗
> brush up on your knowledge of GameSalad while you wait?
>
> Congratulations. Your app is ready! You asked us to build it 2014-12-06 05:33:30 UTC. To start the app the ⊗
> signing process click here

FIGURE 22.6
The feedback messages generated by the Gamesalad servers.

16. **Click** the **Play** button that has become active next to the Publish button. Now give your first published game a try!

Tip: Quick Tips

Throughout the publishing process, pop-up tips can be displayed by resting the pointer on any of the question mark icons on the screen. These tips contain useful details about each item and are worth reading.

Note: App Generation

During the process of app generation, Gamesalad is processing your app on its servers to generate the final game file for use on the chosen platform. The speed at which the app is generated will be influenced by the size of the game and by the server load Gamesalad is experiencing at the time.

Publishing to Apple Devices

While it is beyond the scope of this book to describe every step needed to publish on Apple devices, you should familiarize yourself with the Apple portion of Gamesalad's Publishing Portal (see Figure 22.7). You'll see that this section of the portal is very similar to the Gamesalad Arcade portion so you'll go through many of the same steps to publish to Apple devices.

FIGURE 22.7
The iOS Universal section of the publishing portal.

Note: Apple Developer Center

*In addition to the information that will be input through the Gamesalad Publishing Portal, more information will need to be provided to Apple through their Developer Center. Apple's Developer Center is used to manage and add games to the iTunes Store. More information can be found at the URL: **https://developer.apple.com/***

---

iOS Game Types

Gamesalad supports publishing to all of Apples idevices (iPads, iPhones, and iPods) and also supports publishing games as stand alone Macintosh applications. In addition to these options, games can be published as iOS universal applications.

A universal application is one file that can be played on multiple devices. Using the universal option, one game project can be created for the iPad platform and published to be playable on all versions of the iPad and iPhone. When creating a universal game, it is best to start with a file created for the largest possible device, the iPad, and then use the universal option to scale it down to smaller devices. When creating a game for the iPad, you can be confident that as long as the images used for the iPad are high resolution (retina ready images), they will be clear and crisp on all supported Apple devices.

In the details section for Apple idevices, there are required elements in red just like when publishing to the Gamesalad Arcade. However, there are also a few other options that need to be examined, even though they are not indicated in red.

1. **Bundle Identifier:** A bundle identifier is created through Apple's Developer Center. The bundle identifier entered in this box MUST exactly match that one you create at the Apple Developer Center.
2. **Display Name:** This is the name of the game that will be displayed below the icon on the player's device.
3. **Enable Glossy App Icon:** When active, this option will display a highlight on the app's icon to make it appear shiny.
4. **Supported Orientations:** Use the check boxes below the images to indicate what orientations the game has been created to support.
5. **Aspect Ratio Adjustment:** Choosing one of these three options will determine how the game is displayed; in other words, if it is played on a device with a different aspect ratio from how the project was created. The next section of this chapter covers aspect ratio in more detail.
6. **Custom Loading Image:** Use this area to add a custom-loading image to the game. This image will be displayed on-screen when the game first launches.
7. **Service Configuration:** Pro users are able to use this section to control ad placement and multiplayer options for their games.

iOS Universal Aspect Ratio
As mentioned above, there are three aspect ratio adjustment options available when publishing a project as an iOS Universal Application. These adjustments determine how the game will look when it is played on a device with a different aspect ratio rather than the ratio at which it was created.

Tip: Aspect Ratio
The aspect ratio of a device or image describes the proportional relationship between its width and height. It is often referred to by two numbers separated by a colon. For example, the aspect ratio of an iPad is 4:3 while the iPhone 6 is 16:9.

Aspect Ratio Options:

» **Overscan:** This will crop the game's scene in order to fit the game into different aspect ratios.

» **Letterbox:** This will keep the original aspect ratio of the game and fill any unused space on-screen with the background color of the scene.

» **Stretch:** This will literally stretch, or squeeze, the game on-screen to fit the new aspect ratio.

Once all of the requirements have been satisfied, use the buttons at the top of the details section to generate, sign, and download the app for submission to Apple (see Figure 22.8).

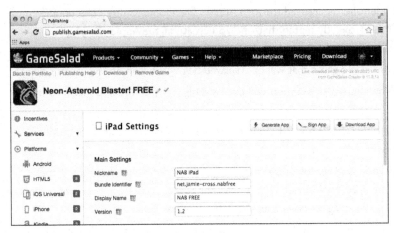

FIGURE 22.8
The Generate App, Sign App and Download App buttons.

Summary

In this chapter, you learned about the Gamesalad Publishing Portal. You learned how to log into your portfolio and how the portfolio organizes and keeps a backup copy of your published projects. You then learned how to use the title, categories, and details sections of the portal to add a new game to your portfolio. You also discovered how to publish the game. Afterwards, you experimented with the portal by publishing one of your projects to the Gamesalad Arcade. You completed the chapter by learning about the requirements to publish to Apple's mobile and desktop devices.

Chapter 23
Improving The Games

In This Chapter You Will Learn:

» How to improve the Pachinko game and make it mobile-ready

» How to improve the Space Shooter game and make it mobile-ready

» How to improve the Box Breaker game and make it mobile-ready

» How to improve the Geometry Runner game and make it mobile- ready

In this chapter, you will make updates to each of the four games you have created while reading this book. These improvements will add features to each game and make sure each game can be played on a mobile device. First, you will add scorekeeping and a GUI to the Pachinko game. Next, you will update the Space Shooter game by adding mobile-friendly controls and special explosion effects to the alien ships. Afterwards, you will add an animated splash screen to the Box Breaker game. Finally, you will finish the hour by adding splash and "game over" scenes to Geometry Runner.

Note: Updated Games

The updated, mobile-ready version of each game is available in the Book Assets Folder for Chapter 23.

Pachinko

The first game you created was a Pachinko style game. Since Gamesalad treats a mouse click as a touch event when a game is published on a mobile device, the controls of this game are already mobile-ready. Since that is the case, you'll make a few improvements to the game so it feels more complete and polished.

Improvements

When you created the Pachinko game in Chapter 5, all of the actors already had their behaviors attached and you just placed them on-screen. Now that you have learned Gamesalad inside and out, you'll be able to create the following improvements from scratch.

Scoring

There will be three different types of score "cups" in the game: one will award the player 25 points, one will award 50 points, and one will award no points.

1. **Open** the file named "Pachinko-Mobile Starter" from the Assets Folder for Chapter 23.
2. Add a new empty Actor to the list of Actors and name it "score 25."
3. Open the Actor Editor and change the Alpha Value under Color to .25. Uncheck Moveable under the Physics settings.
4. Add a Display Text Behavior and make it read:
   Text: 25 » Size: 15 » Color: Gray
5. Make a copy of this Actor and name the copy "score 50." Open this actor's Editor and change the Text Value of the Display Text Behavior to "50."
6. Make a copy of this Actor and name the copy "score –." Open this actor's Editor and change the Text Value of the Display Text Behavior to "–."
7. Return to the Stage and place two copies of the "score 25" actor on the stage.
8. **Double-Click** one of the copies and change the Position and Size to:
   Position (41,31) » Size (81,24)
9. **Double-Click** the other copy and change its Position and Size to:
   Position (438,30) » Size (83,24)
10. Return to the Stage and place two copies of the "score –" actor on the stage.
11. **Double-Click** one of the copies and change the Position and Size to:
    Position (141,30) » Size (81,24)
12. **Double-Click** the other copy and change its Position and Size to:
    Position (337,30) » Size (78,24)
13. Return to the Stage and place a copy of the "score 50" actor on the stage and change its Position and Size to:
    Position (240,31) » Size (77,24)

Preview the game and you'll now see the score cups placed between each of the dividers at the bottom of the stage (see Figure 23.1).

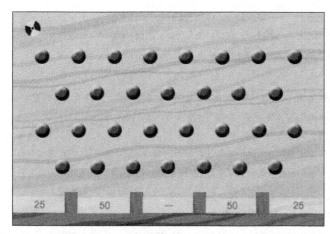

FIGURE 23.1
Score 'cups' added to the Pachinko game.

With the score cups added, the next step is to add to the score value once the ball lands in one of the cups.

1. Open the Ball Actor Editor and add a new Rule to the behaviors list. Name this rule "check for score value."
2. Create a condition for the rule that reads:
    Attribute: self.Motion.Linear Velocity.Y » equals (=) » 0
3. Nest another Rule in this Rule and name it "score 25." Create a condition for the rule that reads:
    Actore receives event » overlaps or collides » with » actor of type » score 25
4. Nest two Change Attribute Behaviors in this Rule and set the first one to read:
    Change Attribute: game.score » To: game.score+25
5. Make the second Change Attribute Behavior read:
    Change Attribute: self.ballDead » To: true
6. Make a copy of the "score 25" Rule and place it below the current "score 25" Rule. Rename it as "score 50."
7. Change this new Rule's condition to read:
    Actor receives event » overlaps or collides » with » actor of type » score 50
8. Update the nested Change Attribute to increase game.score by 50.
9. Make a copy of the "score 50" Rule and place it below the current "score 50" Rule. Rename it as "score –."

10. Change this new Rule's condition to read:
    Actor receives event » overlaps or collides » with » actor of type » score −

11. Delete this rule's nested Change Attribute Behavior that adds to the game.score attribute.

If you were to preview the game now, you would not see any difference. Even though the score is being updated, there is no GUI to display that information to the player. In the following steps, you'll fix that.

1. Return to the Stage and add a new empty Actor to this list of Actors. Name this Actor "score display."

2. Open the Actor Editor for this new Actor, change the Alpha Value to 0, and uncheck Moveable.

3. Add a Display Text Behavior and use the Expression Editor to update it to read:
   Text: "Score:\32"..game.score » Size: 20 » Color: Black

4. Return to the Stage and place a copy of this Actor on-screen. Update its Position and Size to:
   Position (43,300) » Size (56,31)

5. In the Actors Tab, make a copy of the "score display" Actor and rename it as "balls display."

6. Open this Actor's Editor and update the Display Text Behavior to read:
   Text: "Balls:\32"..game.balls

7. Return to the Stage and place a copy of this Actor on-screen, updating its Position and Size to:
   Position (420,300) » Size (53,34)

Preview the game and you'll see that when a ball stops in a score cup, the on-screen GUI is updated with the correct information. However, the ball does not reset once it has stopped moving. You'll fix that now.

1. Open the Actor Editor for the Ball Actor and add a new Rule named "ball dead" to the Behaviors List.

2. Create a condition for this Rule that reads:
   Attribute: » self.ballDead » is » true

3. Nest two Change Attribute Behaviors and a Destroy Behavior within the rule.

4. Update the first Change Attribute Behavior to read:
   Change Attribute: game.balls » To: game.balls-1

5. Update the second Change Attribute Behavior to read:
   Change Attribute: self.ballDead » To: false

6. Add a Destroy Behavior below the second Change Attribute Behavior.

Note: Pachinko Behaviors

Originally, the Pachinko game was "pre-created" for you since at the time you had not learned enough details about Gamesalad to create the game on your own. Now that you have almost completed this book, you should be able to read through the rules and behaviors of the game and understand how all of those behaviors work to make the game function correctly.

Other Improvements

There are a lot of other improvements that could be made to the Pachinko game, including:

» Add a splash screen

» Add pegs with different physics settings so the ball bounces more or less when it hits them

» Add scoring multipliers

» Add a "game over" screen

Space Shooter

The second game you created was the Space Shooter game. To make this game mobile-ready, you'll need to add touch controls on the screen to control the actions of the player's ship.

Mobile Updates

The desktop version of this game is controlled using the keyboard. There are key presses to move the player's ship up, down, left, and right. There's also a key press to fire the ship's cannon. You'll need to add control buttons on the stage to control each one of those actions in the mobile version of the game.

To begin updating the Space Shooter game, open the version named "Space Shooter Mobile Starter" from the Assets Folder for Chapter 23. This version of the game contains additional images you will need to update the original game.

1. Use the images named "up," "down," "left," "right," and "fire" in the images tab to create five new Actors.

2. Create a game level Integer Attribute named "direction" and leave the default value as **0**.

3. Next, create a game level Boolean Attribute named "shoot" and leave the default value as **false** (an unchecked box).

4. Return to the Actors Tab and open the "right" Actor's Editor.

5. Add a Rule to the Behaviors list and create a condition that reads:
    Actor receives event » touch » is » inside

6. Nest a Change Attribute Behavior in the Rule and set it up to read:
   Change Attribute: game.direction » To: I

7. Copy this Change Attribute Behavior and place it in the Otherwise section of the Rule.

8. Change the value I to a **0** in the copied version of the Change Attribute Behavior (see Figure 23.2).

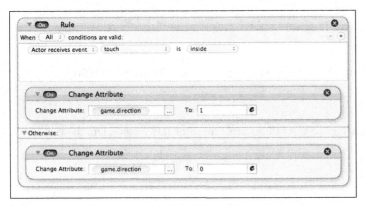

FIGURE 23.2
The completed Rule for the "right" Actor.

9. Copy this entire Rule to the clipboard by choosing **Copy** from the **Edit Menu** (**Edit » Copy**).

10. Open the "down" Actor's Editor and **Paste** a copy of the Rule from the clipboard (**Edit » Paste**).

11. Updated the nested Change Attribute to read:
    Change Attribute: game.direction » To: 2

12. Open the "left" Actor's Editor and **Paste** a copy of the Rule from the clipboard.

13. Update the nested Change Attribute to read:
    Change Attribute: game.direction » To: 3

14. Open the "up" Actor's Editor and **Paste** a copy of the Rule from the clipboard.

15. Update the nested Change Attribute to read:
    Change Attribute: game.direction » To: 4

16. Open the "fire" Actor's Editor and **Paste** a copy of the Rule from the clipboard.

17. Update the Rule's condition to read:
    Actor receives event » touch » is » pressed

18. Change the first Change Attribute Behavior to read:
    Change Attribute: game.shoot » To: true

19. Finally, change the second Change Attribute Behavior (in the Otherwise section) to read:
    Change Attribute: game.shoot » To: false

Note: Touch is pressed vs. Touch is inside

When using "touch is pressed" to create on-screen buttons, the player will need to lift their finger off of the button and touch again to trigger an action. When using "touch is inside," the player will not have to lift their finger and re-touch the screen to trigger an action. Instead, they can simply slide their finger from button to button.

Next, you'll need to place the new buttons on the stage. You can place them anywhere you like or follow the example in Figure 23.3 below.

FIGURE 23.3
On screen control buttons placed on the Stage.

So far, you have added the buttons to the screen and added the necessary behaviors to each button, but none of them will actually work yet. You'll need to make a few edits to the hero-ship actor to get them all working as expected.

1. Open the hero-ship Actor Editor and open the Movement Controls Group if it is closed.
2. Make a copy of the Rule named "Move Up" and rename the copy "Move Up Mobile."
3. Change the first condition of this new Rule to read:
    Attribute » game.direction » equals (=) » 4

4. Copy and rename the Move Right, Move Down, and Move Left Rules, just like you did in step 2 for the Move Up Rule.

5. Update the first condition of each Rule as follows:

   Move Right Mobile: **Attribute » game.direction » equals (=) » 1**

   Move Down Mobile: **Attribute » game.direction » equals (=) » 2**

   Move Left Mobile: **Attribute » game.direction » equals (=) » 3**

6. Copy the Rule named "Shoot" and rename the copy as "Shoot Mobile."

7. Change the condition to read:

   Attribute » game.shoot » is » true

The game now has a complete set of controls for use on desktop computers and on mobile devices.

Improvements

There are many improvements that can be made to this game. Since you learned all about particle effects in Chapter 17, you'll use that knowledge and add some cool particle explosions to the game.

In the following steps, you'll create a single explosion actor and spawn it each time an explosion needs to be displayed on-screen.

1. Create a new, empty Actor and name it "explosion."

2. Open the Actor's Editor and change its Alpha Color setting to **0**.

3. Add a Timer Behavior to the Behaviors List and set it to read:

   For » 0.2 seconds » check Run to Completion

4. Nest a Particles Behavior in the Timer and set the tabs up like so:

   A. Spawn Rate:

   Number of Particles: 200 » Particle Startup Time: 0.2 » Particle Lifetime: 1

   B. Velocity/Position:

   Direction: random(0,359) » Speed: random(200,400)

   C. Size:

   Size: 4 » Size changes to » Target Size: 0.0 » Duration: 1

   D. Color:

   Color: Yellow » Color changes to » Target color: green » Duration: .5

   E. Image:

   Choose the image named "particle" from the drop-down menu.

5. Add another Timer Behavior below the first and set it to read:
   After » 1 seconds
6. Nest a Destroy Behavior in the Timer Behavior.

Now that the explosion actor has been created, it will need to be triggered to display at the right times. The explosion will be triggered when the alien ships have been hit by the player's shot.

1. Open the Actor Editor for the alien-1 Actor and find the Rule named "Shot by the Hero."
2. Nest a Spawn Actor Behavior above the other two Behaviors already nested in this Rule.
3. From the Actor Drop-Down menu choose "explosion."
4. Copy this Spawn Actor Behavior and open the Actor Editor for the alien-2 Actor.
5. Find the Rule named "Shot by the Hero" and paste the Spawn Actor Behavior at the top of the Rule's Behaviors.

Now, when one of the shots fired by the player hits an alien, the alien will be destroyed and the explosion will spawn. You can use this same spawn actor behavior to trigger other explosions in the game by pasting it into the appropriate Rules.

Other Improvements
There are lots of other improvements that can be made to the Space Shooter game, including:

» Add a main menu scene
» Add a win/loss scene
» Add sound effects
» Add additional enemy types
» Add weapon upgrades
» Add additional combat areas like another planet or outer space

Box Breaker
As you may recall, the third game, Box Breaker, was created using touch events to control the breaking of the boxes and the touching of the "pause" and "replay" buttons—this game is ready to publish on a mobile device as it stands. There is nothing additional that needs to be done to the controls to make it mobile-ready. Even though it can be published to a mobile device as it is, there are certainly some things that could be done to make the game feel more complete and polished.

Improvements

To add some polish to the game, you'll add an animated title screen and return the game to the title screen once the player has successfully completed all of the levels.

Open the project titled "Box Breaker Mobile Starter" from within the Assets Folder for Chapter 23. To create the animated splash screen, you are going to use some of the actors that have already been created for the game.

1.   Navigate to the Scenes Tab and add a new Scene to the project.
2.   If the new Scene is not already the first Scene on the list, move it there and name it "Title."
3.   Open the Title Scene's Stage Editor, navigate to the Scene Tab, and change the Height of this Scene to **640**.
4.   Update the Gravity Y Setting in the Scene Tab to **400**.
5.   Return to the Stage and add and center a copy of the "background" Actor to the lower half of the Stage.
6.   Add a copy of the "stone" Actor on the Stage and change its Size to (**480,32**) and change its Position to (**240,16**).
7.   Add several copies of the "wood-cracked" Actor in the top half (black area) of the Stage (see Figure 23.4).

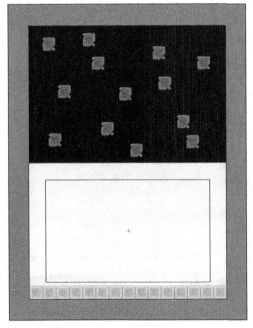

FIGURE 23.4
The background stage for the title scene of Box Breaker.

8. Create a new empty Actor named "Title" in the Actors Tab.

9. Change the Alpha Color Value of this Actor to **0.5** and uncheck Moveable in the Physics Settings.

10. Drag a Display Text Behavior into the Behaviors List and set it up to read:

    Text: Box Breaker » Size:60 » Color: Dark Blue

11. Return to the Actors Tab and make a copy of the "Title" actor. Rename this copy "Play Button."

12. Open the "Play Button" Actor Editor and update the Display Text Behavior to read:

    Text: Play » Size: 30

13. Add a Rule to the Behaviors List and create a condition that reads:

    Actor receives event » touch » is » pressed

14. Nest a Change Attribute Behavior in the Rule and make it read:

    Change Attribute: game.total » To: 0

15. Nest a Change Scene Behavior in the Rule and leave its default values selected.

16. Return to the Stage and add the "Title" and "Play Button" actors to the Stage. Feel free to follow the screen shot below (see Figure 23.5) for placement or design your own screen layout.

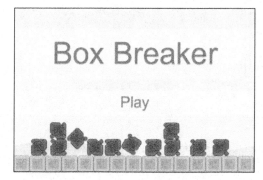

FIGURE 23.5
The text placement on the Box Breaker title screen.

That completes the construction of the title screen. You'll see that when you **Preview** the game, the actors added in the top half of the stage will drop from the sky and bounce on the stone floor at the bottom of the scene, creating an animated splash screen. To complete the improvements, you'll update the final level of the game so it returns to the title screen once the game is complete.

1. Navigate to the final game play Scene in the Scenes Tab, not the Paused scene.

2. Open this scene to enter its Stage Editor and find the "controller" actor that was placed on the pasteboard.

3. **Double-Click** the "controller" Actor that is already placed in the scene and unlock it to make it an instance actor.

4. Find the Change Scene Behavior that is contained in the Rule named "Run this when the level is complete" (see Figure 23.6).

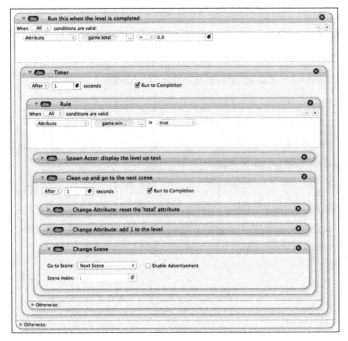

FIGURE 23.6
The "Run this when the level is completed" Rule.

5. Update this Change Scene Behavior by choosing the new Title Scene from the Drop-Down Menu.

Now, when the player finishes the final level, the game will return to the title scene instead of displaying the Pause scene.

Other Improvements

There are a lot of other improvements that can be made to the Box Breaker game, including:

» Add background music
» Add additional levels
» Add additional box types like a bouncy box or an exploding box
» Add a time limit that each level must be completed within
» Add different background environments to add variety to the setting
» Add a particle effect when a box is broken

Geometry Runner

Like Box Breaker, Geometry Runner is already created to be mobile-ready; it was created from the start as an iPhone 6 project that uses touch controls. The jumping action of the player is controlled by a mouse button click, and since Gamesalad treats a mouse click as a touch event when used on a mobile device, the controls are all ready to go mobile.

Improvements

To improve Geometry Runner, you will add a splash screen and life count so the game can end if the player dies too many times.

Splash Screen

You'll create the splash screen first so that when the life count is added in the next section, you'll be able to return the player there when the game is over.

1. Open the file named "Geometry Runner Mobile Starter" from the Assets Folder for Chapter 23.
2. Navigate to the Scenes Tab and add a new Scene to the project. Name the scene "Splash" and drag it to the left of Initial Scene, so it is the first Scene on the list.
3. Add a copy of the "background" Actor to the Stage and center it at:
    Position (333.5, 187.5)
4. Add a copy of the "floor" Actor and place it at the bottom of the Stage.
5. Next, add a copy of the "player" Actor on the floor. **Double-Click** the "player" and unlock it to create an Instance of the "player" Actor.
6. In the Instance Actor, turn off or delete all of the Behaviors except the Play Music Behavior.
7. Use some of the other actors to create a simple scene so the player has some idea what to expect when the game is played. Make sure and leave the top half of the stage open for the title of the game (see Figure 23.7).
8. Use the new image named "GR-Title" that is located in the Images Tab to create a new Actor.
9. Add a Rule to the GR-Title actor and create a condition that reads:
    Actor receives event » touch » is » pressed
10. Nest a Change Scene Behavior in this Rule and choose Next Scene from the Drop-Down menu
11. Place the title Actor in the open area at the top of the Stage.

Preview the game and make sure the title screen performs as expected. The music should play and the game should start when the title graphic is touched or clicked. If things don't work as expected, you'll need to troubleshoot the behaviors you just created.

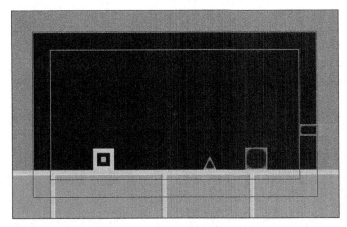

FIGURE 23.7
The splash screen setting.

Life Count

Finally, you'll create the life count so the game can end if the player dies too many times.

Note: Life Count as the Game Controller

In this case, you will be using the life count actor as the game controller—it will watch for when the player has no lives left and end the game. While you have often created a separate actor to control the game, this is not always necessary. Any actor that is on-screen the entire game can act as a "game control" actor.

---

1. Add a new Game Level Integer Attribute. Name it "lives" and give it an initial value of **3**.
2. Next, create a new empty Actor named "Lives" and change its Alpha Color value to **0**.
3. Add a Display Text Behavior to the Behaviors List and set it up like so:
    Text: "Lives:\32"..game.lives » Font: Helvetica » Size: 20
4. Add a Rule to the Behaviors List and create a condition that reads:
    Attribute » game.lives » is less than or equal to (≤) » 0.0
5. Nest a Time Behavior in the Rule and make it read:
    After 1.75 seconds » check Run to Completion
6. Nest a Reset Game Attribute in the Timer.
7. Navigate to the Stage of the "Initial Scene" and place a copy of the "Lives" Actor on Stage. Feel free to place it anywhere as long as it's visible to the player. In the file provided, the actor is placed in the upper left corner of the screen (see Figure 23.8).

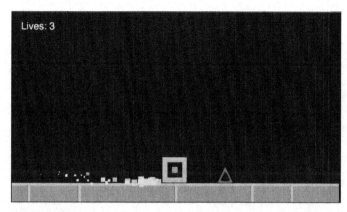

FIGURE 23.8
The "Lives" display actor placed in the game.

8.   Open the "hero" Actor Editor and open the Rule named "Rule: Lose"

9.   Add a Change Attribute to this Rule and set it up to read:
Change Attribute: game.lives » To: » game.lives-1

10.   Open the Timer Behavior named "Timer: Reset The Scene" and delete the Resent Game Behavior that is currently there.

11.   Nest a Change Attribute Behavior in this Timer and set it up to read:
Change Attribute: game.lose » To: » false

12.   Nest a Reset Scene Behavior under the Change Attribute Behavior (see Figure 23.9).

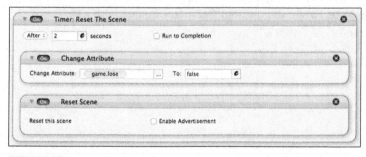

FIGURE 23.9
The updated Timer Behavior.

Note: Reset Game vs. Reset Scene

The reset game behavior will restart the game and send it back to the first scene of the project, resetting any game level attributes to their initial value. This is just like starting a game for the first time by touching the game's icon on your device. The reset scene behavior will restart the current scene and not reset the game level attributes.

Preview the game and playtest it to make sure the player's lives settings function as expected.

Other Improvements

Just like in the other games, there are a lot of things that can be added to make this game even better:

» Add more levels

» Add a moving obstacle

» Add a screen shake effect when the player dies

» Add a save/spawn point in the level

Summary

In this chapter, you made updates to the four games you created while reading this book. First, you updated the Pachinko game by adding scoring and a graphical user interface. Afterwards, you updated the Space Shooter game by adding on-screen touch controls and adding particle effect explosions to the alien ships. From there, you updated the Box Breaker game by adding an animated splash screen and returned the game to this splash screen once it is complete. Finally, you updated Geometry Runner with a life count for the player and also added a splash scene.

Chapter 24
Review and Resources

In This Chapter You Will:

» Review what you have learned

» See what additional resources are available

In this chapter, you'll review everything you've learned about Gamesalad and game development. First, you'll review all of the knowledge you have gathered during the last twenty-three hours. Afterwards, you will learn about some of the various resources that are available online for Gamesalad and game development.

Review

At this point, you've spent at least 23 hours learning how to develop games using Gamesalad. However, it may be helpful to look back and review some of the topics that were covered during that time.

» You learned what game development is and what some of the roles and requirements are for a successful game.

» You learned how to use Gamesalad and how to navigate its interface, including the Inspector and Library palettes.

» You learned how to add scenes to games and how to create multiple game levels and player interface screens.

» You learned about the 2D coordinate system used by Gamesalad to place and control all of the in-game elements.

» You learned how to create and control the appearance of actors using the actor editor.

» You learned the difference between Prototype and Instance actors and when to use each type.

» You learned how to import and use images.

» You learned how to design a game and establish its rules and requirements.

» You learned the importance of playtesting a game and learned some of the things to watch for during testing.

» You learned about the six attribute types that Gamesalad supports and when to use each.

» You learned how to create your own custom game, scene, and actor attributes.

» You learned how to use operators to manipulate attributes.

» You learned how to use Gamesalad's built-in Behaviors to control the actors and actions in a game.

» You learned how to use the Attributes Browser and Expression Editor to further customize Behaviors.

» You learned how to accept player input from the keyboard, the mouse, and touch events.

» You learned how to add music and sound effects to your projects.

» You learned how to add physical properties to actors so they can interact with each other in realistic ways.

» You learned how to control the camera of the game, giving the player a window to your game's world.

» You learned what a Graphical User Interface is and how to create some common GUI elements.

» You learned how to create animations.

» You learned how to create special effects using the Particles Behavior.

» You learned about Tables and what some practical uses of them are.

» You learned what game polish is and how to continually improve your projects.

» You learned about the specifics of developing and publishing a mobile game using Gamesalad.

» You learned how to use Gamesalad's publishing portal.

» You created four mobile games using Gamesalad!

During the course of this book, you have spent a lot of time learning about game development using Gamesalad. You should be proud that now you have the knowledge to create your own custom game projects.

Resources

There are a lot of online resources available to help you to continue learning about Gamesalad and game development.

Gamesalad Resources

Certainly, the first stop in your quest for additional Gamesalad knowledge should be Gamesalad's official website (http://gamesalad.com/). Their website contains a lot of information including a very active and helpful community (http://forums.gamesalad.com/) and detailed tutorials (https://help.gamesalad.com/hc).

There are a lot of other Gamesalad-focused websites as well. Some of the most active include:

» **http://www.jamie-cross.net/**: This is my personal site dedicated to Gamesalad tutorials and information.

» **http://gshelper.com/**: This site hosts a lot of free and paid content, from tutorials to full game templates.

» **http://www.deepblueapps.com/**: This site also hosts lots of free and paid content. They also support other game development platforms outside of Gamesalad.

Game Development Resources

As you have no doubt learned while reading this book, there is a lot more to game development than learning any single software package. The websites listed below offer great information about game development, from general game development articles to game creation tutorials.

» http://gamedevelopment.tutsplus.com/

» http://www.gamasutra.com/

» http://www.gamedev.net/

» http://www.reddit.com/r/gamedev/

Asset Creation Resources

Every game needs a lot of assets besides the rules and behaviors that make everything work. To create a successful game, you'll also need to create lots of graphics and sounds. Below is a list of some common software used to create game assets.

» **Adobe Photoshop** (https://www.adobe.com/products/photoshop.html): Commonly used for raster graphics creation, Photoshop is a professional program and its price reflects that.

» **GIMP** (http://www.gimp.org/): GIMP is a freeware equivalent of Adobe Photoshop. If you're on a budget, this software is certainly worth trying.

» **Adobe Illustrator** (https://www.adobe.com/products/illustrator.html): Illustrator is a vector graphics program and like Photoshop, it is a professional illustration package.

» **Inkscape** (https://inkscape.org/): Inkscape is the equivalent of a free version of Illustrator for developers on a budget.

» **Adobe Flash** (https://www.adobe.com/products/flash.html): While frames of animation can be created in any of the above software packages, a lot of developers like to use a dedicated animation package to create animations. Like the other Adobe products, Flash is a professional level software package.

» **FlipBook Lite** (http://www.digicelinc.com/flipbook.htm):, FlipBook is not free like some of the above packages; however, it is an inexpensive animation package worth checking out.

» **Audacity** (http://audacity.sourceforge.net/): This is a free, open source, audio recorder and editor.

» **GarageBand** (https://www.apple.com/mac/garageband/): Apple's GarageBand is a great tool for creating your own sound effects, soundtracks, and music loops.

» **as3sfxr** (http://www.superflashbros.net/as3sfxr/): This is an awesome online sound editor for creating classic 8-bit sound effects.

Pre-made Assets

It's nice to learn how to create your own graphics and sounds, but not everyone is an artist or has the time to create all of the assets for their games themselves. Luckily, there are a lot of websites online where you can purchase or even download free assets.

Note: Asset Usage Rights

Before downloading purchased or free assets from any online sites, make sure you have read and understood the usage rights for each asset. Every site offers different rights; don't assume an asset from one site has the same usage rights as a similar asset from a different site.

» **http://marketplace.gamesalad.com/:** This is the official Gamesalad Marketplace that contains images, animations, audio files, and full game templates.

» **http://opengameart.org/:** This site offers a collection of image, animation, and audio files for use in games.

» **http://www.freesound.org/:** This site offers a searchable database of audio files for use as sound effects and soundtracks.

» **http://cgtextures.com/:** This site has a lot of files that can be used to create 2D or 3D images.

» **http://www.dreamstime.com/, http://www.bigstockphoto.com/** and **http://www. fotolia.com/:** All offer many stock photos and illustrations for sale.

» **http://www.shockwave-sound.com/:** This site offers a library of searchable audio files.

» **http://audionautix.com/:** This site has a nice library of free music files that are searchable by genre and mood.

Summary

In this chapter you reviewed what you have learned about Gamesalad and game development so far. Afterwards, you were introduced to some online resources that can be used to continue your Gamesalad education. Then you were introduced to many online game development related resources including software packages for creating images and sounds. Finally, you reviewed some online resources where you can find pre-made game assets.

Freelance GameSalad® Developer

Template modifications
Bought a template and needs some modifications to it? From image swaps or App Purchase set ups to level builds and power ups. We love modifiying your template to your needs!

Full Game Builds
We love turning your game ideas into reality. Let us help you develop your idea into a fully functional working game ready for store release. From design through to app store deployment. We cover it all.

Custom Templates
Can't find the right template to build off? Let us build you a custom template to start you off! Maybe you want to sell a template on the marketplace? We build exclusive Templates that you can resell!

Bug Fixing
Have you developed a bug that you just can't find or fix? Let us do the hard work and fix it for you!

Re-Skins
Have a template and want new art made for it? Let us re-skin it for you and create your own masterpiece!

ginga gaming

freelance@gingagaming.com

www.gingagaming.com

GameSalad® and the GameSalad® Logo are trademarks of GameSalad® Inc.

CPSIA information can be obtained at www.ICGtesting.com
Printed in the USA
LVOW03s2318010915

452480LV00008B/107/P